MW00887537

Vocabulary Workbook for SSAT & ISEE (Lower / Middle)

54 Tests with 2500 words covering Synonyms / Antonyms / Blanks / Double Blanks / Spellings / Homonyms / Analogies

By

B Butler

<u>Copyright Notice</u>

All rights reserved.
Do not duplicate or redistribute in any form.

How to use this Workbook

This workbook has 54 Tests, and each test consists of 27 varied questions to test your vocabulary.

The tests cover over 2500 words that frequently appear in the SSAT (Elementary/Middle) and ISEE (Lower/Middle) Examination.

Each set should be done in <u>10 minutes</u>.

Top Tips To learn new words;

1. **Read Regularly**: Grab different kinds of reading materials like books, magazines, and online articles. When you read, you'll bump into new words and see how they're used, which is a cool way to remember them.

2. **Use Flashcards**: How about making some flashcards with new words and their meanings? It's a neat and hands-on way to memorize vocabulary.

3. **Word of the Day**: Let's start a 'word of the day' routine. Each day, we'll learn a new word. You can do this at home or even in class.

4. **Interactive Games**: Have you tried word games like Scrabble, Boggle, or crossword puzzles? They're super fun and they help you learn new words without even realizing it.

5. **Writing Exercises**: Try writing stories or journal entries using the new words you learn. It's a great way to understand how to use these words in different situations.

6. **Use Technology**: There are so many cool apps and websites just for learning new words. They've got quizzes and activities that are perfect for you.

7. **Visual Aids**: Ever tried using mind maps or word trees? They help you remember words and what they mean by linking them to images or diagrams.

8. **Encourage Curiosity**: Whenever you stumble upon a new word, look it up! Find out what it means and how to use it. It's a great way to learn on your own.

9. **Discussion and Usage**: Chat about the new words you learn and try to use them when you talk every day. It really helps in remembering them.

10. **Create a Vocabulary Notebook**: How about keeping a special notebook for new words? Write down the word, its meaning, and maybe even a sentence using it.

11. **Themed Vocabulary Lists**: You can make lists of words that are all about a topic you're interested in. It makes learning them more fun and relevant.

12. **Practice Pronunciation**: It's not just about knowing what a word means, but also how to say it.

13. **Join a Book Club or Discussion Group**: Talking about books and topics with friends can be really motivating and helps you learn.

14. **Role-Playing Games**: Let's pretend! Using new words in role-playing scenarios is a practical and entertaining way to practice.

15. **Incorporate Multisensory Learning**: We all learn differently, so why not try activities that use your sight, hearing, and maybe even movement? It can make learning stick better.

Remember, learning new words is like unlocking new levels in a game. Each word gives you more power to express yourself. Have fun with it!

Tips for doing well in timed tests

1. Watch the Clock: Remember, these tests are timed. Don't get bogged down on a single question. If you're stuck, it's okay to move on and come back to it later.

2. Read Instructions Carefully: This one's super important. Make sure you understand what's being asked. For instance, don't mix up antonyms with synonyms. A simple misread can lead to a bunch of wrong answers, so pay close attention!

3. Strategies for Synonym/Antonym Questions:

Understand the Word in Question: First, make sure you understand the word you're being asked to find a synonym for. If you know the meaning, great. If not, try to infer it from its root, prefix, or suffix.

Eliminate Obvious Non-Matches: Look at the answer choices and immediately rule out any words that you know don't match the meaning of the target word.

Consider Contextual Clues: If the word is used in a sentence, use the context to guide you. The surrounding words often give hints about its meaning.

Narrow Down Choices: Among the remaining options, look for the word that most closely matches the meaning of the target word. If you're stuck between two choices, compare them directly to see which one is a better fit.

4. Strategies for Fill-in-the-Blanks:

The top strategy for solving fill-in-the-blank multiple choice questions is *contextual analysis:*

Read the Entire Sentence: Before looking at the options, read the entire sentence to understand the overall meaning and flow. This sets the stage for what type of word you're looking for.

Identify the Sentence's Structure: Pay attention to the grammatical structure. Is the missing word likely to be a noun, verb, adjective, etc.? This can significantly narrow down your choices.

Look for Contextual Clues: Analyze the sentence for any clues about the word's meaning. Other parts of the sentence might hint at whether the word should indicate contrast, continuation, cause and effect, etc.

Predict the Word Type and Meaning: Before looking at the choices, try to predict the type of word and its meaning based on the sentence's context. This helps you approach the options with a more focused perspective.

Evaluate Each Option: Go through each choice and mentally place it in the blank. Does it make sense both grammatically and contextually?

Eliminate Clearly Wrong Answers: Cross out any options that are clearly incorrect. This simplification can make the right choice more apparent.

Re-read the Sentence with Your Choice: After you select an answer, read the sentence again with your choice in place to ensure it flows naturally and maintains the sentence's intended meaning.

Remember, these tests are not just about knowing the right answers but also about having smart test-taking strategies.

Good luck for the tests that follow, you've got this!

Set 1

A. Synonyms in context: Select the correct answer from the options provided.

1. To <u>swivel</u> in the seat
A) straight   B) stationary   C) fixed   D) stable   E) pivot

2. To <u>mimic</u> an accent
A) genuine   B) original   C) imitate   D) authentic   E) novel

3. To achieve <u>balance</u> on one foot
A) imbalance   B) uneven   C) unstable   D) equilibrium   E) lopsided

4. To <u>animate</u> a character
A) inanimate   B) deaden   C) enliven   D) pacify   E) bore

5. To <u>compress</u> a file
A) expand   B) stretch   C) diffuse   D) scatter   E) condense

6. To play a <u>farcical</u> character
A) serious   B) factual   C) absurd   D) reasonable   E) logical

7. To endure <u>maltreatment</u>
A) care   B) help   C) comfort   D) abuse   E) soothe

8. To be <u>reliant</u> on family
A) independent   B) self-sufficient   C) autonomous   D) self-reliant   E) dependent

B. Sentence Completion – Missing Word

Select the correct answer from the options provided.

1. The sales figures have been _____ for the past quarter.
A) rampant   B) threatening   C) rambling   D) flagging

2. I _____ people who cheat in games.
A) despise   B) respect   C) appreciate   D) approve

3. The weather was _____ all day, so we stayed indoors.
A) attractive   B) dreary   C) stimulating   D) fascinating

4. The museum relies on _____ from wealthy donors to fund its exhibitions.
A) patronage   B) antagonism   C) obstruction   D) resistance

5. The teacher asked the students to control their laughter during class, as it was becoming loud and _____.
A) suppressed   B) soft   C) disruptive   D) restive

C. Homonyms

From the list below, fill in the blanks.

flee	flea	heal	yard	heel	arm

1. A unit of linear measure equal to three feet   _____

2. To make someone or something healthy again   _____

3. A piece of ground adjoining a building or house   _____

4. A part of the body that connects the shoulder and the hand   _____

5. To run away from danger or trouble   _____

6. A branch of an organization   _____

7. To prepare a weapon for action or use   _____

8. An insect that lives on animals and sucks their blood   _____

9. A large, open enclosure where animals are kept   _____

10. The back part of the foot below the ankle   _____

D. Analogies

Select the correct answer from the options provided.

1   JOCUND is to CHEERFUL as
A) clarity is to ambiguity
B) openness is to secrecy
C) plain-spoken is to evasive
D) gloomy is to sullen
E) directness is to indirectness

2   CANDOR is to EVASION as
A) sad is to despondent
B) transparency is to opacity
C) mournful is to melancholy
D) sorrowful is to dejected
E) downcast is to dispirited

3   WHEEL is to CAR as
A) wing is to canoe
B) paddle is to bird
C) rowboat is to oars
D) vessel is to rudder
E) sail is to ship

4   INFECTION is to FEVER as
A) injury is to accident
B) bruise is to blow
C) trauma is to shock
D) fracture is to fall
E) wound is to cut

Set 2

A. Synonyms

Select the word that most closely matches the meaning of the word provided.

1. ABANDON
A) desert   B) support   C) cherish   D) maintain   E) protect

2. BENEVOLENT
A) cruel   B) malicious   C) wicked   D) kind   E) mean

3. CONCISE
A) brief   B) wordy   C) verbose   D) rambling   E) prolix

4. DIVERSE
A) uniform   B) varied   C) identical   D) homogenous   E) consistent

5. HAUGHTY
A) humble   B) modest   C) meek   D) respectful   E) arrogant

6. ANTIDOTE
A) poison   B) remedy   C) venom   D) disease   E) infection

7. SYNTAX
A) error   B) mistake   C) flaw   D) grammar   E) confusion

8. ZEPHYR
A) breeze   B) storm   C) hurricane   D) blizzard   E) tornado

B. Sentence Completion - Double Blanks

Select the correct answer from the options provided.

1. The _____ of the new shopping mall was so crowded that many shoppers decided to go elsewhere for a less _____ experience.

A) location...empty   B) vicinity...chaotic   C) district...peaceful   D) region...populated

2. As she brushed against the plant, a _____ ran up her arm, causing her to _____ in pain.

A) prickle...yelp   B) sting...sharp   C) itch...persistent   D) tingle...tingling

3. The government's decision to_____ strict regulations on the use of plastic bags was met with _____ reactions from the public.

A) enforce...popular   B) implement...saluted   C) apply...settled   D) impose...upset

4. Despite the _____ weather, they decided to take a _____ walk along the beach to enjoy the fresh air.

A) leisurely...relaxing   B) chilly...brisk   C) slow...weakening   D) gentle...soothing

C. Antonyms

Pick the word that means the opposite or near opposite of the word provided.

1. REQUIRED
A) demanded   B) needed   C) noncompulsory D) expected   E) enforced

2. REFINERY
A) dump   B) plant   C) mill   D) machine   E) smelter

3. MEANINGFUL
A) significant   B) important   C) valuable   D) relevant   E) pointless

4. BEREAVEMENT
A) grief   B) joy   C) loss   D) mourning   E) distress

5. GLOWER
A) scowl   B) frown   C) glare   D) smile   E) snarl

6. INSCRIBE
A) write   B) erase   C) etch   D) carve   E) imprint

7. PRECIPITATE
A) hasten   B) accelerate   C) delay   D) cause   E) induce

8. ILLUMINATE
A) light up   B) brighten   C) enlighten   D) clarify   E) darken

D. Synonyms – Spelling

Complete the synonym of the word in **bold**.

1. **harbinger**   h__ r__ ld

2. **accelerate**   exp__ d__ te

3. **request**   ap__ e__ l

4. **repulsive**   di__ gu__ ti__ g

5. **incapable**   u__ __ ble

6. **rhythm**   t__ m__ o

7. **verdict**   se__ te__ ce

Set 3

A. Synonyms in context: Select the correct answer from the options provided.

1. To have a <u>peculiar</u> nature
A) normal   B) typical   C) eccentric   D) regular   E) conform

2. To make <u>stylistic</u> choices in art
A) aesthetic   B) basic   C) simple   D) stark   E) sparse

3. To feel <u>anger</u> rise up
A) calm   B) peaceful   C) relaxed   D) patient   E) rage

4. To tell a <u>parable</u>
A) reality   B) allegory   C) truth   D) certainty   E) fact

5. To have a <u>faulty</u> appliance
A) flawless   B) perfect   C) defective   D) functional   E) robust

6. To <u>stimulate</u> the economy
A) numb   B) deaden   C) pacify   D) bore   E) activate

7. To leave a <u>legacy</u>
A) inheritance   B) closure   C) cessation   D) stoppage   E) halt

8. To be <u>liable</u> for damages
A) exempt   B) clear   C) absolved   D) responsible   E) freed

B. Sentence Completion – Missing Word

Select the correct answer from the options provided.

1. The politician's speech was full of _____ and didn't make much sense.
A) gibberish   B) appreciation   C) perception   D) logic

2. The actor's _____ was evident in his arrogant behavior on set.
A) labor   B) struggle   C) conceit   D) toil

3. The shy student was _____ to answer the question in front of the class.
A) conclusive   B) hesitant   C) critical   D) convincing

4. The teacher was _____ when she found out that her students had vandalized the classroom.
A) thrilled   B) contented   C) satisfied   D) livid

5. The newspaper reporter got a big _____ when she uncovered a major scandal involving the city's mayor.
A) scoop   B) problem   C) notice   D) work

C. Homonyms

From the list below, fill in the blanks.

flue	faun	hole	fawn	whole	flu

1. A figure in Roman mythology _____

2. A young deer _____

3. To court favor in a cringing or flattering manner _____

4. An opening through something _____

5. A complete amount or sum _____

6. Short form of influenza _____

7. An enclosed passage for smoke or air _____

8. Make a perforation or puncture _____

9. Having all its proper parts or components _____

10. Light yellowish brown color _____

D. Analogies

Select the correct answer from the options provided.

1 VACCINE is to IMMUNIZE as
A) splint is to shield
B) raincoat is to immobilize
C) intruder is to fence
D) bandage is to protect
E) buckle is to seatbelt

2 FOX is to CUNNING as
A) beaver is to powerful
B) lion is to industrious
C) owl is to wise
D) ant is to transformative
E) bee is to solitary

3 AUSTERE is to HARSH as
A) plain is to complex
B) sparse is to fertile
C) disciplined is to lenient
D) restrained is to free
E) gentle is to tender

4 ASCENDING is to DESCENDING as
A) rising is to falling
B) elevating is to increasing
C) lowering is to sinking
D) mounting is to placing
E) lifting is to carrying

Set 4

A. Synonyms

Select the word that most closely matches the meaning of the word provided.

1. RANT
A) praise   B) compliment   C) rave   D) admire   E) flatter

2. TANTALIZE
A) repel   B) deter   C) tempt   D) dissuade   E) prevent

3. PANORAMA
A) close-up   B) detail   C) fragment   D) part   E) vista

4. HUNCH
A) doubt   B) uncertainty   C) skepticism   D) intuition   E) mistrust

5. SPLASH
A) squelch   B) plenty   C) excess   D) surplus   E) glut

6. DULL
A) exciting   B) boring   C) thrilling   D) lively   E) vibrant

7. FORTHRIGHT
A) deceitful   B) dishonest   C) lying   D) honest   E) false

8. UNHAPPY
A) happy   B) miserable   C) content   D) satisfied   E) joyful

B. Sentence Completion - Double Blanks
Select the correct answer from the options provided.

1. After hours of hiking, they finally found a _____ water source to _____ their thirst.

A) drinkable...quench   B) beverage...refresh   C) clean...dehydrate   D) satisfying...purified

2. The journalist's _____ towards a particular political party was evident in his reporting, leading to accusations of _____.

A) inclination...neutral   B) prejudice...unbiased   C) bias...unfairness   D) impartiality...balanced

3. Despite their differences, they were able to _____ each other's viewpoints and work together towards a _____ goal.

A) reject...divergent   B) ignore...opposing   C) intolerant...conflicting D) accept...common

4. The hiker followed a clear _____ through the _____ forest, knowing where it would lead.

A) message...direct   B) strange...route   C) trail...mysterious   D) passage...ambiguous

C. Antonyms

Pick the word that means the opposite or near opposite of the word provided.

1. DEFRAY
A) pay   B) cover   C) settle   D) finance   E) charge

2. DEVALUE
A) depreciate   B) appreciate   C) lower   D) cheapen   E) degrade

3. DIMINISH
A) decrease   B) reduce   C) increase   D) shrink   E) decline

4. FULLNESS
A) completeness   B) emptiness   C) plenitude   D) richness   E) satisfaction

5. RESTORATIVE
A) healing   B) curative   C) therapeutic   D) harmful   E) invigorating

6. BOLSTER
A) support   B) weaken   C) reinforce   D) boost   E) uphold

7. DISBELIEVE
A) doubt   B) distrust   C) question   D) skepticize   E) consider

8. UNWORLDLY
A) innocent   B) knowing   C) naive   D) idealistic   E) unexperienced

D. Synonyms – Spelling

Complete the synonym of the word in **bold**.

1. **suspect**   m__ s__ ru__ t

2. **delay**   po__ tp__ ne

3. **testy**   ir__ ita__ le

4. **hazard**   d__ ng__ r

5. **veneer**   c__ at__ ng

6. **enumerate**   it__ m__ ze

7. **quandary**   di__ fic__ lt__

Set 5

A. Synonyms in context: Select the correct answer from the options provided.

1. To cause a <u>debacle</u>
A) success   B) triumph   C) achievement   D) disaster   E) accomplishment

2. To maintain a <u>pristine</u> reputation
A) dirty   B) tainted   C) immaculate   D) stained   E) corrupted

3. To <u>slump</u> in the chair after a long day
A) straighten   B) perk up   C) rise   D) collapse   E) stiffen

4. To clear the <u>undergrowth</u> before planting
A) barrenness   B) vegetation   C) desolation   D) aridity   E) sterility

5. To <u>denunciate</u> the author's work
A) praise   B) compliment   C) laud   D) criticize   E) acclaim

6. To <u>swath</u> a wound in bandages
A) unwrap   B) expose   C) reveal   D) uncover   E) wrap

7. To man the <u>turret</u> and fire
A) surrender   B) retreat   C) gun   D) capitulate   E) yield

8. To take <u>precautions</u> against something
A) risk   B) hazard   C) safeguard   D) jeopardize   E) compromise

B. Sentence Completion – Missing Word

Select the correct answer from the options provided.

1. Despite his best efforts, he couldn't help but feel the weight of his _____ performance.
A) exemplary   B) laudable   C) failing   D) exceptional

2. The liquid _____ in the tank as the truck rumbled down the road.
A) sloshed   B) slithered   C) edged   D) wriggled

3. The speaker's words _____ the audience, leaving them captivated.
A) boiled   B) mumbled   C) spoke   D) riveted

4. The politician's message was so _____ that it was impossible to understand his true intentions.
A) garbled   B) concise   C) clear   D) precise

5. He walked down the street with a/an _____ step, whistling a cheerful tune.
A) solemn   B) listless   C) hesitant   D) jaunty

C. Homonyms

From the list below, fill in the blanks.

sale	peal	coarse	sail	peel	course

1. Having a rough or uneven surface   _____

2. A series of lectures or lessons on a particular subject   _____

3. A large piece of fabric used to propel a ship   _____

4. To travel by boat   _____

5. The loud ringing of bells   _____

6. Lacking refinement or good taste   _____

7. To remove the outer layer of something   _____

8. The act of selling something   _____

9. A special discount or offer on goods or services   _____

10. The path or direction something takes   _____

D. Analogies

Select the correct answer from the options provided.

1   AFFINITY is to AVERSION as
A) harmony is to accord
B) attraction is to repulsion
C) reliability is to coherence
D) hope is to optimism
E) giving is to charitable

2   TOUCHSCREEN is to SMARTPHONE as
A) engine is to cycle
B) violin is to strings
C) stage is to mic
D) building is to foundation
E) monitor is to computer

3   OVERWATERING is to ROT as
A) under-stimulation is to interest
B) undercooling is to hyperactivity
C) underfeeding is to stunted growth
D) underdressing is to composed
E) underthinking is to surprise

4   MISCONCEPTION is to FALLACY as
A) truth is to inaccuracy
B) sincerity is to dissimilarity
C) confidence is to nervousness
D) accuracy is to precision
E) belief is to distrust

Set 6

A. Synonyms

Select the word that most closely matches the meaning of the word provided.

1. FATAL
A) harmless   B) benign   C) lethal   D) safe   E) healthy

2. INDUCE
A) prevent   B) inhibit   C) deter   D) stop   E) cause

3. DISUNITY
A) discord   B) unity   C) agreement   D) concord   E) peace

4. IDYLLIC
A) awful   B) blissful   C) terrible   D) horrible   E) atrocious

5. SNIFFLE
A) laugh   B) giggle   C) chuckle   D) snivel   E) smile

6. BRUSQUE
A) polite   B) curt   C) gracious   D) civil   E) respectful

7. VERITY
A) lie   B) falsehood   C) fiction   D) deception   E) truth

8. MISREPRESENT
A) preserve   B) maintain   C) distort   D) respect   E) honor

B. Sentence Completion - Double Blanks

Select the correct answer from the options provided.

1. Filled with excitement and _____ for the upcoming event, she could hardly contain her _____.

A) unease...energy   B) anticipation...joy   C) indifference...boredom   D) dread...apprehension

2. The professor's _____ behavior and attire made him a familiar figure on campus, easily distinguished from his more _____ colleagues.

A) flamboyant...reckless   B) reserved...remarkable   C) introverted...lame   D) enigmatic...ordinary

3. A notorious _____ terrorized the neighborhood with his gang, causing _____ among the residents.

A) philanthropist...peace   B) criminal...distress   C) scholar...admiration   D) artist...inspiration

4. The chemist carefully _____ the raw materials, hoping to _____ the essence of the potion.

A) crushed...destroy   B) mixed...abolish   C) heated...purify   D) froze...extinguish

C. Antonyms

Pick the word that means the opposite or near opposite of the word provided.

1. MALADJUSTED
A) dysfunctional   B) disturbed   C) abnormal   D) troubled   E) well-accustomed

2. EXPOUND
A) explain   B) elucidate   C) clarify   D) interpret   E) obscure

3. DEPLOY
A) employ   B) utilize   C) mobilize   D) withdraw   E) activate

4. CLEVERNESS
A) stupidity   B) ingenuity   C) wit   D) skill   E) creativity

5. BROADEN
A) widen   B) expand   C) enlarge   D) narrow   E) diversify

6. IMMOBILIZED
A) paralyzed   B) rallied   C) frozen   D) halted   E) fixed

7. SLITHER
A) glide   B) slide   C) sneak   D) creep   E) jump

8. ROGUE
A) conformist   B) villain   C) rascal   D) rebel   E) outlaw

D. Synonyms – Spelling

Complete the synonym of the word in **bold**.

1. **condone**   d__ sre__ ard

2. **contemplate**   p__ nde__

3. **crevice**   __ rac__

4. **brevity**   co__ cis__ ne__ s

5. **paraphernalia** eq__ ip__ en__

6. **copycat**   im__ ers__ n__ tor

7. **eradicate**   __ lim__ na__ e

Set 7

A. Synonyms in context: Select the correct answer from the options provided.

1. To <u>instigate</u> an uprising
A) calm   B) provoke   C) soothe   D) appease   E) placate

2. To <u>entrance</u> someone with beauty
A) bore   B) repel   C) disgust   D) annoy   E) mesmerize

3. To <u>flail</u> one's arms
A) flap   B) restrain   C) steady   D) calm   E) soothe

4. To be <u>vindictive</u> towards someone
A) spiteful   B) merciful   C) generous   D) kind   E) benevolent

5. To see <u>luminous</u> stars in the night sky
A) radiant   B) dull   C) dark   D) gloomy   E) murky

6. To fall into <u>disrepute</u>
A) honor   B) esteem   C) disgrace   D) reputation   E) fame

7. To be in <u>quiescence</u> for centuries
A) activity   B) eruption   C) agitation   D) dormancy   E) liveliness

8. To <u>befit</u> something perfectly
A) mismatch   B) suit   C) contrast   D) differ   E) disagree

B. Sentence Completion – Missing Word
Select the correct answer from the options provided.

1. The children were _____ with excitement as they reached the park.
A) dejected   B) animated   C) indifferent   D) bored

2. Looking back solemnly, he realized that his decision to leave had been a/an _____ one.
A) blank   B) melancholy   C) regrettable   D) jolly

3. The rock was so _____ that it seemed impossible to break it apart.
A) fragile   B) brittle   C) flexible   D) unyielding

4. The doctor recommended that she gets a/an _____ done for her health.
A) checkup   B) vaccine   C) medicine   D) shot

5. The sudden storm _____ the town, leaving behind a trail of destruction.
A) passed over   B) avoided   C) eluded   D) befell

C. Homonyms

From the list below, fill in the blanks.

paws	pause	one	tie	well	won

1. The number 1 _____

2. The feet of an animal, such as a dog or cat _____

3. To rise to the surface and flow out _____

4. In good health or a satisfactory condition _____

5. The past tense of "win" _____

6. A single person or thing _____

7. A piece of string or cord used for fastening or tying something _____

8. To stop or delay something _____

9. South Korean currency _____

10. To achieve the same score as another competitor _____

D. Analogies

Select the correct answer from the options provided.

1   MICROSCOPE is to EXAMINE as
A)   brush is to painter
B)   compass is to deviate
C)   telescope is to observe
D)   display is to projector
E)   dictionary is to writer

2   PRECIPITATION is to DOWNPOUR as
A)   earthquake is to vibration
B)   explosion is to combustion
C)   condensation is to compost
D)   air movement is to gale
E)   decay is to dew

3   SERENE is to TRANQUIL as
A)   chaotic is to disorderly
B)   spontaneous is to meticulous
C)   adaptable is to unyielding
D)   versatile is to unchanging
E)   fluid is to fixed

4   FICKLE is to STEADFAST as
A)   barren is to parched
B)   lumbering is to clumsy
C)   flexible is to rigid
D)   stagnant is to decaying
E)   grating is to cacophonous

Set 8

A. Synonyms

Select the word that most closely matches the meaning of the word provided.

1. RECORD
A) erase   B) forget   C) document   D) neglect   E) destroy

2. IRIDESCENT
A) dull   B) shimmering   C) drab   D) dim   E) dark

3. FAÇADE
A) reality   B) truth   C) honesty   D) essence   E) front

4. REFUTE
A) disprove   B) support   C) agree   D) validate   E) accept

5. DART
A) linger   B) dawdle   C) loiter   D) crawl   E) dash

6. WASTE
A) grow   B) wither   C) thrive   D) develop   E) strengthen

7. DEBUG
A) break   B) corrupt   C) damage   D) fix   E) impair

8. INSIST
A) yield   B) demand   C) concede   D) surrender   E) obey

B. Sentence Completion - Double Blanks
Select the correct answer from the options provided.

1. The government treated the mysterious object as if it were an extraterrestrial _____, questioning its _____ and purpose.

A) creature...origins   B) artifact...historical   C) entity...unknown   D) weapon...destructive

2. The prisoners were forced to _____ before the emperor, a symbol of their complete _____ to his authority.

A) laugh...disrespect   B) fight...rebellion   C) bow...submission   D) argue...disagreement

3. The project encountered several _____ delays due to unforeseen difficulties, causing _____ for the team.

A) unexpected...relief   B) minor...convenience   C) planned...relaxation   D) significant...frustration

4. As he contemplated his unfortunate situation, he wondered whether it was simply _____ or a cruel twist of _____.

A) reality...imagination   B) bad luck...fate   C) freedom...choice   D) logic...reason

C. Antonyms

Pick the word that means the opposite or near opposite of the word provided.

1. DOTE
A) adore   B) cherish   C) pamper   D) hate   E) spoil

2. FRAY
A) fight   B) battle   C) conflict   D) wear   E) mend

3. IMPORTANT
A) significant   B) trivial   C) vital   D) crucial   E) valuable

4. EVACUATE
A) vacate   B) depart   C) flee   D) withdraw   E) occupy

5. TROPHY
A) failure   B) award   C) honor   D) accolade   E) laurel

6. REPUTE
A) reputation   B) disgrace   C) fame   D) renown   E) prestige

7. LACERATE
A) tear   B) cut   C) slash   D) wound   E) heal

8. PERPETUAL
A) eternal   B) temporary   C) constant   D) infinite   E) ceaseless

D. Synonyms – Spelling

Complete the synonym of the word in **bold**.

1. **duration**   p __ ri __ d

2. **unmanageable**   di __ fic __ lt

3. **scold**   __ eb __ ke

4. **opportune**   t __ me __ y

5. **breach**   br __ a __

6. **consume**   d __ pl __ te

7. **leverage**   a __ van __ ag __

Set 9

A. Synonyms in context: Select the correct answer from the options provided.

1. To have an <u>excess</u> of money
A) lack   B) deficiency   C) scarcity   D) shortage   E) surplus

2. To <u>recall</u> a fact
A) forget   B) ignore   C) remember   D) neglect   E) disregard

3. To be <u>bitten</u> by mosquitoes
A) stung   B) avoid   C) prevent   D) protect   E) deter

4. To <u>dedicate</u> oneself to something
A) devote   B) abandon   C) desert   D) forsake   E) renounce

5. To be made of <u>combustible</u> material
A) fireproof   B) flammable   C) incombustible   D) resistant   E) impervious

6. To be a <u>titan</u> in his field
A) dwarf   B) giant   C) pygmy   D) runt   E) shrimp

7. To be on one end of a <u>spectrum</u>
A) fixed   B) range   C) certain   D) precise   E) exact

8. To <u>seclude</u> oneself from others
A) join   B) isolate   C) socialize   D) interact   E) connect

B. Sentence Completion – Missing Word

Select the correct answer from the options provided.

1. The young contestant was _____ with nerves before taking the stage.
A) composed   B) indifferent   C) overwrought   D) unfazed

2. She looked forward to the _____ of spring, when the world would come alive again.
A) departure   B) retreat   C) arrival   D) removal

3. The dancer moved with a/an _____ grace that mesmerized the audience.
A) clumsy   B) stiff   C) uncoordinated   D) lithe

4. He spoke with a/an _____ voice, unsure of how his words would be received.
A) confident   B) timid   C) boastful   D) eloquent

5. The professor's lecture on _____ was fascinating, shedding light on the complexities of human language.
A) history   B) mathematics   C) linguistics   D) geography

C. Homonyms

From the list below, fill in the blanks.

steal	illicit	strike	elicit	steel	bank

1.   A refusal to work as a form of protest   _____

2.   To nick something that belongs to someone else   _____

3.   To draw out information or a response from someone   _____

4.   A financial institution   _____

5.   The edge of a river, lake, or canal   _____

6.   Not permitted by law or morality   _____

7.   A strong, hard metal alloy   _____

8.   To hit or attack someone or something forcefully or violently   _____

9.   A set or series of similar things, especially machines or devices   _____

10. A sudden attack, typically a military one   _____

D. Analogies

Select the correct answer from the options provided.

1   REFREE is to WHISTLE as
A)   gardener is to scalpel
B)   musician is to choreography
C)   painter is to brush
D)   writer is to books
E)   chef is to cook

2   GREGARIOUS is to SOCIABLE as
A)   fearless is to frightened
B)   pioneer is to conformist
C)   aloof is to withdrawn
D)   rule-breaker is to stickler
E)   showy is to modest

3   SEEDLING is to SAPLING as
A)   oak is to acorn
B)   caterpillar is to chrysalis
C)   star is to nebula
D)   flower is to bud
E)   moth is to cocoon

4   AUDACIOUS is to TIMID as
A)   bold is to cowardly
B)   hermit is to recluse
C)   solitary is to self-contained
D)   guarded is to circumspect
E)   stoic is to introspective

Set 10

A. Synonyms

Select the word that most closely matches the meaning of the word provided.

1. BARRICADE
A) open   B) clear   C) block   D) unblock   E) release

2. REVIVAL
A) renewal   B) decay   C) deterioration D) collapse   E) death

3. ZOMBIE
A) alive   B) living   C) conscious   D) aware   E) undead

4. WHOLESOME
A) harmful   B) unhealthy   C) healthy   D) sickly   E) rotten

5. ONEROUS
A) burdensome   B) light   C) simple   D) effortless   E) pleasant

6. INANE
A) sensible   B) rational   C) logical   D) silly   E) wise

7. MANIFEST
A) hidden   B) evident   C) unclear   D) vague   E) secret

8. LOFTY
A) low   B) humble   C) modest   D) grand   E) ordinary

B. Sentence Completion - Double Blanks

Select the correct answer from the options provided.

1. The scientists could only _____ about the cause of the phenomenon, as there was no concrete evidence to _____ any single theory.

A) conjecture...confirm   B) settle...explain   C) research...analyze   D) speculate...support

2. He yearned for something more than the fleeting pleasures of life, something with _____, a sense of _____ and lasting meaning.

A) temporality...brevity   B) uncertainty...doubt   C) change...alteration   D) permanence...stability

3. The _____ aircraft glistened under the hangar lights, ready to embark on its next _____ journey.

A) mundane...ordinary   B) perilous...safe   C) majestic...adventurous   D) routine...scheduled

4. The doctor's _____methods and bizarre remedies were met with skepticism and accusations of _____.

A) unorthodox...quackery   B) effectiveness...succes   C) expertise...skill   D) innovation...genius

C. Antonyms

Pick the word that means the opposite or near opposite of the word provided.

1. INEXORABLE
   A) relentless   B) unstoppable   C) inevitable   D) implacable   E) flexible

2. ENDURE
   A) bear   B) succumb   C) withstand   D) tolerate   E) persevere

3. HACK
   A) cut   B) chop   C) slash   D) splice   E) gash

4. DOUBTFUL
   A) skeptical   B) certain   C) uncertain   D) hesitant   E) suspicious

5. GRACIOUS
   A) courteous   B) kind   C) polite   D) benevolent   E) rude

6. DEVISE
   A) invent   B) create   C) copy   D) plan   E) concoct

7. MONETARY
   A) financial   B) nonmonetary   C) fiscal   D) pecuniary   E) currency

8. FRUGALITY
   A) thrift   B) extravagance   C) prudence   D) saving   E) moderation

D. Synonyms – Spelling

Complete the synonym of the word in **bold**.

1. **clearance**   a__pro__al

2. **residence**   dw__ll__ng

3. **grievance**   co__pla__n__

4. **menace**   d__ng__r

5. **ably**   __apa__ly

6. **imitate**   __mula__e

7. **insensitivity**   in__if__er__nce

Set 11

A. Synonyms in context: Select the correct answer from the options provided.

1. To be <u>sulky</u> after losing
A) moody   B) happy   C) bright   D) sunny   E) joyful

2. To bleed <u>profusely</u>
A) scarce   B) abundantly   C) measly   D) sparse   E) limited

3. To <u>prattle</u> on about the day
A) silence   B) quiet   C) hush   D) chatter   E) still

4. To <u>overcome</u> an opponent
A) lose   B) beat   C) concede   D) yield   E) succumb

5. To see a <u>tendril</u> in a plant
A) straighten   B) curl   C) smooth   D) level   E) even

6. To have a <u>meager</u> salary
A) ample   B) abundant   C) plentiful   D) generous   E) scanty

7. To be <u>slothful</u> at work
A) diligent   B) lazy   C) active   D) energetic   E) vigorous

8. To be <u>spiritual</u> in beliefs
A) secular   B) worldly   C) material   D) profane   E) religious

B. Sentence Completion – Missing Word

Select the correct answer from the options provided.

1. The once vibrant city now lay dormant, covered in a thick layer of _____ after the volcanic eruption.
A) confetti   B) glitter   C) ash   D) manure

2. The council members met to discuss the _____ of the new law.
A) ruminate   B) contemplate   C) debate   D) implementation

3. The vandal _____ the statue with graffiti, leaving behind a permanent mark.
A) restored   B) refurbished   C) defaced   D) repaired

4. The old house had a/an _____ smell to it, a reminder of its neglect and decay.
A) dank   B) pleasant   C) fresh   D) sweet

5. He was nervous and began to _____ as he stood before the crowd.
A) aplomb   B) confident   C) falter   D) poise

C. Homonyms

From the list below, fill in the blanks.

idle	idol	weather	stick	whether	idyll

1.   The atmospheric conditions in a particular place   _____

2.   A thin piece of wood that has fallen or been cut off a tree   _____

3.   Not working or doing anything   _____

4.   Expressing a doubt or choice between alternatives   _____

5.   A staff or a cane used as an aid in walking   _____

6.   A serene or peaceful scene   _____

7.   To push or thrust something into or through something else   _____

8.   A statue or image of a god or revered deity   _____

9.   A person or thing that is greatly admired   _____

10.   To attach or adhere something with a glue   _____

D. Analogies

Select the correct answer from the options provided.

1   WING is to AIRPLANE as
A)   oar is to helicopter
B)   horse is to hoof
C)   snake is to tail
D)   road is to car
E)   rudder is to boat

2   FERVENT is to ZEALOUS as
A)   fickle is to constant
B)   indifferent is to apathetic
C)   bubbly is to glum
D)   social butterfly is to loner
E)   flashy is to understated

3   DROUGHT is to ARIDITY as
A)   flood is to erosion
B)   obscurity is to notoriety
C)   harmony is to noise
D)   anarchy is to order
E)   lava is to eruption

4   GENEROUS is to STINGY as
A)   content is to serene
B)   chatty is to rambling
C)   tidy is to finicky
D)   selfless is to greedy
E)   respected is to revered

Set 12

A. Synonyms

Select the word that most closely matches the meaning of the word provided.

1. UNABATED
A) persistent   B) stopping   C) ending   D) diminishing   E) decreasing

2. NARRATE
A) listen   B) hear   C) observe   D) watch   E) tell

3. REFRACTORY
A) obedient   B) stubborn   C) docile   D) flexible   E) cooperative

4. AFFLUENT
A) poor   B) wealthy   C) destitute   D) penniless   E) impoverished

5. REGRESS
A) progress   B) advance   C) improve   D) retreat   E) grow

6. INCOMPETENT
A) competent   B) incapable   C) skilled   D) proficient   E) expert

7. TARNISH
A) polish   B) clean   C) brighten   D) stain   E) improve

8. ADVERSARIAL
A) friendly   B) amicable   C) cooperative   D) supportive   E) hostile

B. Sentence Completion - Double Blanks
Select the correct answer from the options provided.

1. Observing the chaos from a distance, she felt surprisingly _____ and _____ by the emotional turmoil around her.

A) involved...kind   B) calm...unaffected   C) concerned...nervous   D) dazed...self-reliant

2. The violinist's _____ playing transported the audience to a world of beauty and serenity, leaving them spellbound by the _____.

A) discordant...tune   B) melodic...discord   C) technical...virtuosity   D) rhythmic...melody

3. The speaker's _____ remarks ignited a _____ of controversy, dividing the audience into opposing factions.

A) incendiary...firestorm   B) witty...humor   C) banal...kind   D) persuasive...agreement

4. Fueled by the crowd's enthusiastic _____ and their own surging confidence, the team carried the game's _____ into the second half.

A) silence...caution   B) applause...momentum   C) criticism...defeat   D) jeers...hesitation

C. Antonyms

Pick the word that means the opposite or near opposite of the word provided.

1. STURDY
A) strong   B) fragile   C) robust   D) durable   E) stable

2. NOBLE
A) honorable   B) dignified   C) aristocratic   D) virtuous   E) dishonorable

3. SCREECH
A) scream   B) whisper   C) yell   D) howl   E) squawk

4. PRIMARY
A) secondary   B) principal   C) chief   D) foremost   E) leading

5. FACTIOUS
A) divisive   B) dissenting   C) rebellious   D) contentious   E) unified

6. CENSOR
A) approve   B) suppress   C) restrict   D) edit   E) condemn

7. LIKENESS
A) similarity   B) resemblance   C) image   D) difference   E) copy

8. CONFIRM
A) authorize   B) discredit   C) refute   D) endorse   E) approve

D. Synonyms – Spelling

Complete the synonym of the word in **bold**.

1. **bizarre**   s__ra__ge

2. **helpful**   b__ne__ic__al

3. **impulsive**   s__ont__neo__s

4. **criticism**   __isap__ro__al

5. **upset**   di__tr__ss__d

6. **genre**   __ate__or__

7. **respite**   r__l__ef

Set 13

A. Synonyms in context: Select the correct answer from the options provided.

1. To <u>spray</u> the paint
A) absorb   B) soak   C) sponge   D) squeegee   E) spurt

2. To be an <u>uninteresting</u> read
A) fascinating   B) boring   C) intriguing   D) exciting   E) thrilling

3. To be in <u>turmoil</u>
A) order   B) chaos   C) harmony   D) stability   E) calmness

4. To strive for <u>perfection</u>
A) imperfection   B) fault   C) flawlessness   D) blemish   E) error

5. To have a <u>lump</u> on the head
A) depression   B) dent   C) hollow   D) bulge   E) pit

6. To be <u>permissive</u> with children
A) lenient   B) rigid   C) stern   D) severe   E) harsh

7. To be an <u>inveterate</u> smoker
A) occasional   B) sporadic   C) rare   D) infrequent   E) habitual

8. To <u>defy</u> orders from superiors
A) obey   B) comply   C) disobey   D) follow   E) submit

B. Sentence Completion – Missing Word

Select the correct answer from the options provided.

1. Her stern voice _____ silence, and the chattering students instantly quietened down.
A) submitted   B) followed   C) commanded   D) conformed

2. The vast rangeland _____ out before them, an endless sea of green and gold.
A) unperturbed   B) undisturbed   C) untroubled   D) stretched

3. The lawyer served as the _____ for the defendant, presenting their case to the court.
A) mouthpiece   B) critic   C) judge   D) magistrate

4. The baby's sudden _____ pierced the quiet of the night, startling everyone.
A) giggle   B) coo   C) squeal   D) sigh

5. The children played hide-and-seek among the thick and _____ trees of the forest.
A) lush   B) barren   C) stunted   D) sparse

C. Homonyms

From the list below, fill in the blanks.

cereal	tide	serial	tied	bat	stamp

1. Relating to, consisting of, or arranged in a rank, or row _____

2. The regular rise and fall of the sea level _____

3. A grain food such as wheat, oats, or rice _____

4. A small piece of paper used to prepay postage _____

5. Fastened, attached, or bound _____

6. Appearing in successive parts or numbers _____

7. Performing a series of similar acts over a period _____

8. A wooden or metal club used to hit a ball in some sports _____

9. A mark or impression made by imprinting _____

10. A nocturnal flying mammal _____

D. Analogies

Select the correct answer from the options provided.

1   FLIPPANT is to SOLEMN as
A)   unyielding is to constant
B)   bright is to scintillating
C)   regular is to unending
D)   pleasant is to euphonious
E)   irreverent is to pious

2   ALPACA is to WOOL as
A)   cotton plant is to pearl
B)   oyster is to boll
C)   goose is to down
D)   maple is to berry
E)   grapevine is to sap

3   DRUPE is to PEACH as
A)   citrus is to apple
B)   pome is to orange
C)   endocarp is to raspberry
D)   drupelet is to pit
E)   legume is to peanut

4   PERSISTENT is to TENACIOUS as
A)   carefree is austere
B)   combative is to peacemaking
C)   disrespectful is to submissive
D)   fleeting is to ephemeral
E)   rowdy is to hushed

Set 14

A. Synonyms

Select the word that most closely matches the meaning of the word provided.

1. ITEMIZE
A) group   B) combine   C) merge   D) list   E) unify

2. HUMBLE
A) arrogant   B) modest   C) vain   D) boastful   E) haughty

3. BIZARRE
A) normal   B) usual   C) common   D) strange   E) familiar

4. DEFINE
A) confuse   B) explain   C) complicate   D) distort   E) mislead

5. TRANCE
A) alertness   B) awareness   C) clarity   D) lucidity   E) daze

6. OUTRAGE
A) delight   B) anger   C) pleasure   D) satisfaction   E) happiness

7. COMMEND
A) praise   B) blame   C) condemn   D) rebuke   E) censure

8. ENTERPRISE
A) inertia   B) stagnation   C) idleness   D) laziness   E) venture

B. Sentence Completion - Double Blanks
Select the correct answer from the options provided.

1. As the pupils of his eyes began to _____ in the dim light, he _____ to discern the figures moving in the shadows.

A) dilate...strained   B) constrict...brightness   C) flutter...confusion   D) contract...darkness

2. The triumphant return of the explorers was met with joyous _____ and a parade of celebratory _____.

A) scorn...ridicule   B) whispers...suspicion   C) silence...disapproval   D) fanfare...rejoicing

3. He was ostracized by his community for his _____ behavior and views, deemed too _____ for their conservative society.

A) common...adaptable   B) deviant...eccentric   C) acceptable...normative   D) admirable...desirable

4. The winter wind howled with _____ fury, whipping the snow into a swirling blizzard and making travel nearly _____.

A) gentle...pleasant   B) harsh...impossible   C) calm...relaxing   D) soothing...comfortable

C. Antonyms

Pick the word that means the opposite or near opposite of the word provided.

1. KEEPSAKE
A) souvenir   B) memento   C) token   D) trash   E) reminder

2. JUDICIOUS
A) wise   B) imprudent   C) sensible   D) judge   E) discreet

3. PEEVISH
A) cheerful   B) cranky   C) grumpy   D) petulant   E) fretful

4. MAKEUP
A) cosmetics   B) foundation   C) lipstick   D) mascara   E) natural

5. IMPERATIVE
A) essential   B) optional   C) necessary   D) crucial   E) vital

6. FUME
A) anger   B) fury   C) rage   D) seethe   E) calm

7. REPUGNANT
A) disgusting   B) attractive   C) abhorrent   D) loathsome   E) offensive

8. HIDEAWAY
A) refuge   B) landmark   C) sanctuary   D) shelter   E) hideout

D. Synonyms – Spelling

Complete the synonym of the word in **bold**.

1. **engulf**   su__me__ge

2. **container**   r__ser__oir

3. **warning**   c__ut__on

4. **sentimental**   e__oti__na__

5. **lucrative**   pr__fit__ble

6. **seriously**   e__rn__stly

7. **unpretentious**   un__ss__mi__g

Set 15

A. Synonyms in context: Select the correct answer from the options provided.

1. To be <u>permissible</u> under the law
A) allowable   B) prohibited   C) illegal   D) banned   E) unlawful

2. To cause <u>discord</u> among friends
A) harmony   B) peace   C) agreement   D) conflict   E) concord

3. To <u>cackle</u> like a hen
A) cry   B) laugh   C) weep   D) wail   E) moan

4. To <u>grip</u> the handle tightly
A) release   B) loosen   C) drop   D) let go   E) grasp

5. To <u>incubate</u> an egg
A) freeze   B) hatch   C) chill   D) ice   E) frost

6. To be <u>exuberant</u> after winning
A) depressed   B) miserable   C) sad   D) gloomy   E) ecstatic

7. To sing with a <u>soulful</u> voice
A) soulless   B) heartfelt   C) emotionless   D) indifferent   E) apathetic

8. To have an <u>imperial</u> history
A) humble   B) modest   C) meek   D) majestic   E) unassuming

B. Sentence Completion – Missing Word

Select the correct answer from the options provided.

1. The presence of security cameras served as a powerful _____ to crime.
A) encouragement   B) incentive   C) opportunity   D) deterrent

2. The task seemed _____ at first, but with determination, he managed to overcome it.
A) daunting   B) easy   C) trivial   D) simple

3. The witness testimony _____ the suspect's alibi, leading to their acquittal.
A) contradicted   B) corroborated   C) dismissed   D) refuted

4. The building was constructed with _____ materials, ensuring its longevity and resilience.
A) cheap   B) fragile   C) solid   D) temporary

5. He realized that he had been a/an _____, falling victim to a cleverly planned scam.
A) hero   B) victor   C) beneficiary   D) dupe

C. Homonyms

From the list below, fill in the blanks.

pact	cede	packed	spring	bear	seed

1.   To yield or grant typically by treaty   _____

2.   A formal treaty   _____

3.   The grains or ripened ovules of plants used for sowing   _____

4.   The season after winter   _____

5.   To carry or support something   _____

6.   An agreement or understanding   _____

7.   A large, furry animal   _____

8.   A sudden jump or movement forward   _____

9.   To rank (a contestant) relative to others in a tournament   _____

10. Filled tightly with something   _____

D. Analogies

Select the correct answer from the options provided.

1   IMPEDE is to OBSTRUCT as
A)   sincere is to insincere
B)   open is to secretive
C)   merciful is to vengeful
D)   reasonable is to irrational
E)   facilitate is to ease

2   CHEF is to WHISK as
A)   guitar is to musician
B)   author is to pen
C)   surgeon is to hammer
D)   microscope is to scientist
E)   carpenter is to scalpel

3   CANDID is to DISHONEST as
A)   streamline is to simplify
B)   liberate is to disentangle
C)   truthful is to deceitful
D)   purify is to cleanse
E)   clarify is to illuminate

4   FELINE is to LYNX as
A)   marsupial is to wombat
B)   canine is to chameleon
C)   reptile is to dingo
D)   bird is to horse
E)   equine is to hoopoe

Set 16

A. Synonyms

Select the word that most closely matches the meaning of the word provided.

1. RECLINE
A) sit   B) stand   C) lean   D) erect   E) vertical

2. INFECTED
A) clean   B) contaminated   C) pure   D) healthy   E) cured

3. INSOLENT
A) polite   B) rude   C) courteous   D) humble   E) civil

4. APPROACH
A) depart   B) leave   C) retreat   D) loom   E) withdraw

5. EXQUISITE
A) ugly   B) gorgeous   C) ordinary   D) dull   E) mediocre

6. GROUCHY
A) grumpy   B) happy   C) pleasant   D) friendly   E) amiable

7. DETOUR
A) direct   B) diversion   C) shortcut   D) linear   E) shortest

8. INCOMPLETE
A) complete   B) finished   C) whole   D) perfect   E) unfinished

B. Sentence Completion - Double Blanks

Select the correct answer from the options provided.

1. The peaceful village was thrown into turmoil when a foreign army _____ their land, forcing the villagers to flee in _____.

A) liberated...joy   B) defended...unity   C) invaded...terror   D) aided...relief

2. After months of captivity, they finally experienced the long-awaited _____ from their oppressors, savoring the sweet taste of _____.

A) experiment...liberty   B) trial...judgment   C) deliverance...freedom   D) penalty...regret

3. The island nation relied heavily on the _____ of food and other essential goods, as their own resources were _____.

A) consumption...plentiful   B) export...abundant   C) distribution...available   D) import...limited

4. The doctor's grim diagnosis of a _____ disease left the patient feeling hopeless and _____.

A) terminal...despondent   B) minor...optimistic   C) curable...relieved   D) manageable...strong

C. Antonyms

Pick the word that means the opposite or near opposite of the word provided.

1. ENLIGHTEN
A) educate   B) inform   C) illuminate   D) confuse   E) clarify

2. INTERMEDIARY
A) mediator   B) direct   C) broker   D) agent   E) negotiator

3. AUTHORITY
A) influence   B) power   C) control   D) powerlessness E) territory

4. UNTESTED
A) proven   B) untried   C) novel   D) new   E) innovative

5. KEYNOTE
A) main   B) central   C) dominant   D) fundamental   E) minor

6. FUTILE
A) useless   B) effective   C) hopeless   D) pointless   E) fruitless

7. WISTFUL
A) nostalgic   B) longing   C) melancholy   D) dreamy   E) satisfied

8. VIABLE
A) feasible   B) impossible   C) practical   D) realistic   E) sustainable

D. Synonyms – Spelling

Complete the synonym of the word in **bold**.

1. **skulk**   s__e__k

2. **charm**   ap__e__l

3. **nip**   __inc__

4. **necessitate** r__qui__e

5. **boldness**   c__ura__e

6. **circulate**   __pre__d

7. **summon**   co__v__ne

Set 17

A. Synonyms in context: Select the correct answer from the options provided.

1. To be an <u>immortal</u> being
A) mortal   B) finite   C) perishable   D) transient   E) eternal

2. To be <u>kindred</u> spirits
A) related   B) different   C) dissimilar   D) diverse   E) distinct

3. To have a <u>skimpy</u> meal
A) ample   B) generous   C) inadequate   D) plentiful   E) lavish

4. To be <u>mellow</u> after a glass of wine
A) relaxed   B) nervous   C) anxious   D) stressed   E) agitated

5. To be a <u>counselor</u> at the school
A) client   B) student   C) learner   D) follower   E) adviser

6. To <u>mull</u> over an offer
A) ponder   B) neglect   C) disregard   D) overlook   E) forget

7. To <u>reconcile</u> with a former friend
A) quarrel   B) fight   C) make up   D) dispute   E) clash

8. To <u>hamper</u> someone's progress
A) help   B) assist   C) aid   D) hinder   E) facilitate

B. Sentence Completion – Missing Word

Select the correct answer from the options provided.

1. A deep _____ formed between her brows as she pondered the problem at hand.
A) furrow   B) smile   C) smirk   D) grin

2. The garden was a lush oasis, _____ with life and vibrant colors.
A) scant   B) teeming   C) meagre   D) withered

3. The judge announced a harsh _____ to deter future offenders.
A) reward   B) accolade   C) punishment   D) leniency

4. He spent hours _____ over the meaning of her words, trying to decipher her true intentions.
A) functioning   B) ruminating   C) operating   D) practicing

5. The instructions were so _____ that he felt lost and unsure of what to do.
A) clear   B) precise   C) detailed   D) vague

C. Homonyms

From the list below, fill in the blanks.

sound	birth	week	bill	berth	weak

1.   A place where a ship or boat can moor   _____

2.   Lacking strength or power   _____

3.   The arrival of an offspring   _____

4.   A period of seven days   _____

5.   To bring forth, to give rise to   _____

6.   In good condition; not damaged, injured, or diseased   _____

7.   A thing that can be heard   _____

8.   A piece of paper money   _____

9.   A statement of charges or cost for goods or services   _____

10.   Mentally or intellectually deficient   _____

D. Analogies

Select the correct answer from the options provided.

1   IMPERTINENT is to RESPECTFUL as
A)   turbulent is to chaotic
B)   rambling is to verbose
C)   vindictive is to spiteful
D)   insolent is to courteous
E)   murky is to opaque

2   PIXEL is to IMAGE as
A)   note is to melody
B)   line is to dot
C)   rope is to strand
D)   step is to dancer
E)   writer is to paragraph

3   SUNBURN is to SUN EXPOSURE as
A)   seasickness is to mountain climbing
B)   hypothermia is to cold exposure
C)   altitude sickness is to protection
D)   frostbite is to sailing
E)   heat stroke is to car travel

4   MELODIOUS is to HARMONIOUS as
A)   dull is to unflattering
B)   bright is to blight
C)   noisy is to discordant
D)   sophistic is to bossy
E)   harassed is to exhausted

Set 18

A. Synonyms

Select the word that most closely matches the meaning of the word provided.

1. COMPETENCE
A) incompetence   B) skill   C) ineptitude   D) weakness   E) deficiency

2. CONJURE
A) summon   B) dismiss   C) dispel   D) exorcise   E) eliminate

3. HEADSTRONG
A) flexible   B) compliant   C) obedient   D) docile   E) stubborn

4. RETROSPECT
A) review   B) forecast   C) prediction   D) projection   E) anticipation

5. REPRISAL
A) forgiveness   B) pardon   C) mercy   D) retaliation   E) leniency

6. DISTRUST
A) trust   B) doubt   C) faith   D) belief   E) reliance

7. PREY
A) predator   B) hunter   C) attacker   D) target   E) assailant

8. BOISTEROUS
A) quiet   B) noisy   C) calm   D) peaceful   E) serene

B. Sentence Completion - Double Blanks

Select the correct answer from the options provided.

1. In a dramatic public speech, he _____ his former beliefs and allegiance, declaring his _____ to a new cause.

A) reaffirmed...loyalty   B) renounced...commitment   C) embraced...reception   D) secured...defense

2. The soup was thick and _____ with chunks of vegetables and meat - a _____ meal perfect for a cold winter day.

A) watery...thin   B) cold...light   C) smooth...hearty   D) bland...unappetizing

3. The scientist carefully _____ the material with radiation, hoping to _____ its effects on its molecular structure.

A) examined...study   B) freeze...preserve   C) heat...melt   D) polish...shine

4. The treaty was finally _____ by the Senate, paving the way for its implementation and ushering in a new era of international _____.

A) rejected...opposition   B) ratified...cooperation   C) amended...variation   D) postponed...delay

C. Antonyms

Pick the word that means the opposite or near opposite of the word provided.

1. RUSTIC
A) rural   B) country   C) pastoral   D) simple   E) urban

2. CUNNING
A) naive   B) crafty   C) sly   D) devious   E) shrewd

3. PARTISAN
A) biased   B) loyal   C) devoted   D) impartial   E) one-sided

4. ENCLOSURE
A) cage   B) pen   C) fence   D) opening   E) envelope

5. DEMOLISH
A) destroy   B) wreck   C) build   D) raze   E) smash

6. REDEEM
A) save   B) condemn   C) recover   D) restore   E) atone

7. ENROLL
A) register   B) withdraw   C) sign up   D) admit   E) enlist

8. PREFACE
A) introduction   B) prologue   C) foreword   D) conclusion   E) opening

D. Synonyms – Spelling

Complete the synonym of the word in **bold**.

1. **shun**   a__o__d

2. **smolder**   s__ok__

3. **discount**   re__uct__on

4. **proceed**   __ont__nue

5. **haphazard**   u__pla__ne__

6. **dissatisfy**   di__a__p__int

7. **germinate**   s__ro__t

Set 19

A. Synonyms in context: Select the correct answer from the options provided.

1. To <u>excise</u> the tumor
A) insert   B) remove   C) implant   D) attach   E) append

2. To believe in <u>destiny</u>
A) choice   B) option   C) decision   D) fate   E) alternative

3. To have a <u>fleeting</u> feeling
A) lasting   B) transient   C) enduring   D) eternal   E) infinite

4. To use <u>hyperbole</u> in a story
A) understatement   B) reality   C) exaggeration   D) truth   E) accuracy

5. To be <u>hostile</u> to a stranger
A) friendly   B) amiable   C) cordial   D) pleasant   E) unfriendly

6. To be <u>nefarious</u> in deeds
A) wicked   B) good   C) righteous   D) noble   E) moral

7. To have an <u>inaccuracy</u> in a report
A) accuracy   B) correctness   C) precision   D) exactness   E) error

8. To use a <u>bracket</u> to prop a stand
A) eradicate   B) support   C) erase   D) eliminate   E) discard

B. Sentence Completion – Missing Word

Select the correct answer from the options provided.

1. The smart detective managed to _____ the criminal, catching him and retrieving the stolen cash.
A) outwit   B) befriend   C) assist   D) underestimate

2. With a graceful _____ the athlete landed safely after completing her routine.
A) ascent   B) dismount   C) clap   D) heave

3. The teenager's incessant giggling and spitball barrage left the classroom in a state of _____ chaos.
A) mature   B) responsible   C) immature   D) thoughtful

4. The desert stretched before them in a/an _____ expanse of sand and sun.
A) limited   B) confined   C) endless   D) fragmented

5. Despite their differences, the two cultures managed to _____ peacefully for generations.
A) coexist   B) clash   C) discriminate   D) isolate

C. Homonyms

From the list below, fill in the blanks.

bough	inn	bow	in	pail	pale

1.   A branch of a tree   _____

2.   Lacking color or brightness   _____

3.   To bend the head or body in greeting or respect   _____

4.   A tavern   _____

5.   To express thanks by bending head   _____

6.   Something bent into a simple curve or arc   _____

7.   A bucket   _____

8.   The forward part of a ship   _____

9.   Within a place or area   _____

10. A public house providing accommodation and food   _____

D. Analogies

Select the correct answer from the options provided.

1   HAMMER is to POUND as
A)   screwdriver is to turn
B)   bellows is to bore
C)   drill is to fan
D)   wipe is to squeegee
E)   sculpt is to chisel

2   VIGILANT is to COMPLACENT as
A)   stale is to malodorous
B)   gloomy is to despondent
C)   rigid is to stiff
D)   rambling is to meandering
E)   alert is to inattentive

3   VACANT is to EMPTY as
A)   occupied is to full
B)   graceful is to awkward
C)   diplomatic is to abrasive
D)   determined is to vacillating
E)   productive is to fallow

4   SPORT is to FOOTBALL as
A)   novel is to literature
B)   board game is to chess
C)   python is to code
D)   music is to sing
E)   utensil is to eat

Set 20

A. Synonyms

Select the word that most closely matches the meaning of the word provided.

1. EXHORT
A) discourage   B) deter   C) dissuade   D) urge   E) inhibit

2. ILLUSION
A) reality   B) impression   C) fact   D) certainty   E) clarity

3. RESTRAINT
A) freedom   B) liberty   C) release   D) indulgence   E) control

4. FRAGRANCE
A) odor   B) perfume   C) stench   D) reek   E) foulness

5. RECONDITE
A) clear   B) obvious   C) plain   D) simple   E) obscure

6. GREED
A) generosity   B) charity   C) materialism   D) altruism   E) kindness

7. SYSTEMATIC
A) chaotic   B) random   C) disorderly   D) haphazard   E) orderly

8. COHERE
A) separate   B) stick   C) loosen   D) release   E) divide

B. Sentence Completion - Double Blanks
Select the correct answer from the options provided.

1. The artist's deliberate _____ in the composition of the _____ created a dynamic tension and drew the viewer's attention to specific elements.

A) asymmetry...painting   B) symmetry...disorder   C) equality...reliability   D) order...chaos

2. The ship sent out a distress _____ into the night, hoping it would be intercepted by a passing vessel and lead to their _____.

A) broadcast...influx   B) celebration...joy   C) warning...danger   D) signal...rescue

3. As a willing _____ in the experiment, she agreed to undergo a series of tests to help _____ medical research and potentially improve the lives of others.

A) observer...analysis   B) bystander...curiosity   C) participant...advance   D) critic...judgment

4. The project's _____ was vast, encompassing several countries and requiring the _____ of hundreds of researchers.

A) complexity...detail   B) efficiency...precision   C) simplicity...brevity   D) scope...collaboration

C. Antonyms

Pick the word that means the opposite or near opposite of the word provided.

1. MISUNDERSTAND
A) misinterpret   B) confuse   C) mistake   D) misconstrue   E) comprehend

2. SAFEGUARD
A) protect   B) endanger   C) defend   D) preserve   E) guard

3. UTOPIA
A) paradise   B) ideal   C) heaven   D) dystopia   E) perfection

4. FASTIDIOUS
A) meticulous   B) careless   C) choosy   D) scrupulous   E) finicky

5. ZOOLOGICAL
A) animal   B) faunal   C) wildlife   D) botanical   E) zooid

6. ENTERTAIN
A) amuse   B) bore   C) divert   D) please   E) charm

7. SUBJECTIVE
A) objective   B) biased   C) emotional   D) individual   E) opinionated

8. VACUOUS
A) empty   B) shallow   C) hollow   D) stupid   E) full

D. Synonyms – Spelling

Complete the synonym of the word in **bold**.

1. **scintillate**   __par__le

2. **perpetuate**   m__in__ain

3. **decline**   di__ini__h

4. **persist**   p__rse__ere

5. **poignant**   t__uc__ing

6. **prone**   in__lin__d

7. **protest**   di__sen__

Set 21

A. Synonyms in context: Select the correct answer from the options provided.

1. To <u>wreak</u> havoc
A) prevent   B) cause   C) avert   D) stop   E) hinder

2. To be a <u>miser</u> with the money
A) spender   B) giver   C) donor   D) philanthropist E) hoarder

3. To be <u>autonomous</u> in work
A) independent   B) reliant   C) subordinate   D) controlled   E) regulated

4. To <u>scout</u> for a new location
A) ignore   B) neglect   C) disregard   D) explore   E) shun

5. To be <u>prosaic</u> in speech
A) dull   B) creative   C) imaginative   D) artistic   E) expressive

6. To have <u>diverse</u> opinions
A) uniform   B) similar   C) varied   D) same   E) alike

7. To be <u>slanderous</u> toward rival
A) truthful   B) defamatory   C) factual   D) accurate   E) reliable

8. To have an <u>exodus</u> from a country
A) arrival   B) entry   C) entrance   D) departure   E) admission

B. Sentence Completion – Missing Word

Select the correct answer from the options provided.

1. Her _____ voice cut through the silence, demanding immediate attention.
A) soft   B) whispering   C) strident   D) soothing

2. The once vibrant city had become a/an _____ wasteland, devoid of life and activity.
A) torpid   B) thriving   C) bustling   D) flourishing

3. The old building was a/an _____ of a bygone era, a reminder of the city's rich history.
A) ultramodern   B) futuristic   C) remnant   D) obsolete

4. The company decided to _____ some of its laid-off employees during the busy season.
A) dismiss   B) employ   C) terminate   D) sack

5. They attempted to _____ the old factory, hoping to breathe new life into the abandoned machinery.
A) dismantle   B) destroy   C) reactivate   D) neglect

C. Homonyms

From the list below, fill in the blanks.

yolk	made	maid	yoke	set	book

1. A collection of items that belong together   _____

2. Past tense of "make"   _____

3. A wooden crosspiece by which two draft animals are joined   _____

4. A woman or girl employed to do domestic work   _____

5. The yellow part of an egg   _____

6. A written or printed work   _____

7. How something is arranged, positioned, or fixed   _____

8. To make a reservation   _____

9. To schedule engagements for   _____

10. Unlikely to change   _____

D. Analogies

Select the correct answer from the options provided.

1   KEY is to LOCK as
A)   computer is to mouse
B)   handlebar is to bicycle
C)   faucet is to ring
D)   guitar is to tuner
E)   switch is to light

2   SCIENTIST is to EXPERIMENT as
A)   novelist is to fly
B)   journalist is to subscribe
C)   historian is to document
D)   writer is to public speaking
E)   musicologist is to describe

3   CONCISE is to RAMBLING as
A)   precise is to vague
B)   savage is to feral
C)   lynching is to massacre
D)   hurricane is to tempest
E)   shout is to bellow

4   MILD is to GENTILE as
A)   candid is to evasive
B)   adaptable is to stubborn
C)   peaceful is to chaotic
D)   fierce is to brutal
E)   nuanced is to obvious

Set 22

A. Synonyms

Select the word that most closely matches the meaning of the word provided.

1. HEM
A) center   B) core   C) middle   D) border   E) essence

2. CHALICE
A) cup   B) spoon   C) fork   D) straw   E) tray

3. GROAN
A) cheer   B) rejoice   C) celebrate   D) applaud   E) grunt

4. AUTOCRACY
A) democracy   B) dictatorship   C) collectivism   D) capitalism   E) socialism

5. MERGE
A) separate   B) unite   C) split   D) part   E) scatter

6. DASTARDLY
A) brave   B) cowardly   C) heroic   D) bold   E) fearless

7. UNBLEMISHED
A) fog   B) cloud   C) obscure   D) blur   E) clear

8. EXCLUSIVE
A) inclusive   B) restricted   C) accessible   D) universal   E) common

B. Sentence Completion - Double Blanks
Select the correct answer from the options provided.

1. The accident had caused _____ injury to several people, leaving them with _____ physical and emotional scars.

A) minor...problem   B) transient...wieldy   C) grievous...lasting   D) trivial...brief

2. The candidate carefully considered her _____ on the issue before taking a _____ that would potentially alienate some of her supporters.

A) passion...enthusiasm   B) position...stance   C) uncertainty...doubt   D) apathy...balance

3. The betrayal of his closest friend left him _____ and filled with a deep sense of _____ and distrust.

A) bitter...resentment   B) empower...strength   C) reconcile...pity   D) liberate...joy

4. The hidden entrance to the secret passage was cleverly disguised, lying just _____ your feet, completely _____.

A) beyond...distant   B) beside...adjacent   C) above...over   D) below...unseen

C. Antonyms

Pick the word that means the opposite or near opposite of the word provided.

1. ASSOCIATE
A) connect   B) relate   C) partner   D) detach   E) join

2. PROVOKE
A) incite   B) pacify   C) stimulate   D) anger   E) trigger

3. DRAFTY
A) airtight   B) breezy   C) chilly   D) leaky   E) cold

4. REPRESENTATIVE
A) delegate   B) misleading   C) spokesperson   D) typical   E) symbolic

5. PERSISTENCE
A) perseverance   B) determination   C) endurance   D) feebleness   E) steadfastness

6. INJUSTICE
A) unfairness   B) fairness   C) oppression   D) inequality   E) corruption

7. EFFECT
A) result   B) outcome   C) impact   D) cause   E) influence

8. REVELATION
A) disclosure   B) discovery   C) surprise   D) confession   E) concealment

D. Synonyms – Spelling

Complete the synonym of the word in **bold**.

1. **flawed**   d__fe__tive

2. **convene**   as__em__le

3. **dillydally**   pro__ras__ina__e

4. **suffice**   s__tis__y

5. **exalt**   __lori__y

6. **reoccur**   __epe__t

7. **perilous**   __ang__rou__

Set 23

A. Synonyms in context: Select the correct answer from the options provided.

1. To have an <u>intent</u> to harm
A) accident   B) chance   C) coincidence   D) luck   E) intention

2. To have <u>fidelity</u> to a spouse
A) infidelity   B) loyalty   C) betrayal   D) treachery   E) perfidy

3. To <u>explain</u> the problem
A) confuse   B) obscure   C) clarify   D) perplex   E) mystify

4. To <u>titter</u> at a joke
A) frown   B) scowl   C) glare   D) giggle   E) sneer

5. To <u>explode</u> the bomb
A) detonate   B) deactivate   C) disarm   D) disable   E) dismantle

6. To be <u>weary</u> after the journey
A) energetic   B) tired   C) vigorous   D) alert   E) refreshed

7. To be in an <u>untainted</u> condition
A) tainted   B) corrupted   C) polluted   D) contaminated   E) pure

8. To <u>exult</u> in victory
A) revel   B) grieve   C) lament   D) sorrow   E) regret

B. Sentence Completion – Missing Word
Select the correct answer from the options provided.

1. The patient's _____ movements worried the doctor, indicating a possible neurological issue.
A) smooth   B) controlled   C) spasmodic   D) coordinated

2. The Queen's _____ gesture silenced the entire crowd.
A) tentative   B) hesitant   C) nervous   D) sweeping

3. The mountain stood _____ and unyielding, a constant presence in the valley below.
A) fragile   B) stolid   C) crumbling   D) trembling

4. He greeted his guests with a/an _____ smile, radiating warmth and hospitality.
A) gloomy   B) unwelcoming   C) indifferent   D) lively

5. They needed to _____ their supplies before embarking on the long journey.
A) augment   B) leave   C) donate   D) defer

C. Homonyms

From the list below, fill in the blanks.

case	real	reel	rapt	wrapped	rap

1.   Filled with intense pleasure or interest   _____

2.   Having objective independent existence   _____

3.   An instance or occurrence of something   _____

4.   Covered or enclosed in something   _____

5.   A legal action or a matter to be decided by a court _____

6.   A container or a cover for holding or protecting something _____

7.   Not artificial, fraudulent, or illusory   _____

8.   A large spool used for winding thread or yarn   _____

9.   One of two forms in which an alphabet may be written _____

10. A genre of music   _____

D. Analogies

Select the correct answer from the options provided.

1   FRAGILE is to DELICATE as
A)   fickle is to trustworthy
B)   sturdy is to robust
C)   whimsy is to resolve
D)   moodiness is to composure
E)   unpredictable is to steady

2   EXCESSIVE EXERCISE is to MUSCLE SORENESS
A)   mountain climbing is to comfortable legs
B)   forgetting sunburn is to sunscreen
C)   overeating is to stomachache
D)   burning wax is to melting candle
E)   loud music is to ringing eyes

3   CHILD is to NAIVE as
A)   oak is to graceful
B)   dog is to frail
C)   seedling is to agile
D)   eagle is to weathered
E)   adult is to experienced

4   MERCURIAL is to STEADFAST as
A)   volatile is to stable
B)   enduring is to everlasting
C)   enigma is to uncrackable
D)   roar is to anthem
E)   mirror is to reflective

Set 24

A. Synonyms

Select the word that most closely matches the meaning of the word provided.

1. ENFORCE
A) revoke   B) cancel   C) withdraw   D) annul   E) impose

2. UNRIVALED
A) equaled   B) unmatched   C) rivaled   D) surpassed   E) exceeded

3. TAINT
A) purify   B) cleanse   C) sanitize   D) stain   E) freshen

4. DABBLE
A) experiment   B) master   C) excel   D) perfect   E) expertize

5. BASEMENT
A) attic   B) loft   C) cellar   D) rooftop   E) terrace

6. PROPEL
A) stop   B) halt   C) brake   D) drive   E) hinder

7. AROMATIC
A) odorless   B) fragrant   C) bland   D) foul   E) stinky

8. INEQUALITY
A) equality   B) disparity   C) balance   D) fairness   E) justice

B. Sentence Completion - Double Blanks

Select the correct answer from the options provided.

1. The gathering was a _____ and _____ affair, with friends and family enjoying each other's company without any formal protocol.

A) formal...structured   B) relaxed...casual   C) official...solemn   D) stiff...sore

2. He emphasized his point with a broad _____ of his arm, leaving no room for _____ in his message.

A) gaze...penetrating   B) nod...noncommittal   C) whisper...subtle   D) gesture...ambiguity

3. The government's _____ decision-making process fostered public trust and confidence in its _____.

A) transparent...leadership B) opaque...secretive   C) biased...unfair   D) manipulative...deceitful

4. The _____ expanse of the desert stretched as far as the eye could see, a humbling reminder of the universe's _____ size.

A) vast...immense   B) confined...limited   C) populated...dense   D) familiar...recognizable

C. Antonyms

Pick the word that means the opposite or near opposite of the word provided.

1. IMPEDE
A) hinder   B) facilitate   C) delay   D) block   E) hamper

2. DOMINANT
A) submissive   B) commanding   C) prevailing   D) superior   E) assertive

3. PERCEIVE
A) notice   B) observe   C) sense   D) understand   E) ignore

4. CRAVEN
A) cowardly   B) timid   C) fearful   D) brave   E) frightened

5. PENETRATE
A) enter   B) exit   C) infiltrate   D) perforate   E) invade

6. AESTHETIC
A) beautiful   B) artistic   C) unpleasant   D) elegant   E) stylish

7. UNATTAINABLE
A) impossible   B) unreachable   C) unrealistic   D) inaccessible   E) achievable

8. VINDICATION
A) justification B) defense   C) exoneration   D) conviction   E) validation

D. Synonyms – Spelling

Complete the synonym of the word in **bold**.

1. **soundness**   r__li__b__lity

2. **pertinent**   __ele__ant

3. **endnote**   fo__tn__te

4. **halt**   __au__e

5. **risible**   la__gh__ble

6. **memorandum**   m__s__age

7. **appease**   __la__ate

Set 25

A. Synonyms in context: Select the correct answer from the options provided.

1. To <u>vilify</u> an enemy
A) praise   B) compliment   C) laud   D) extol   E) slander

2. To have the <u>nerve</u> to talk back
A) timidity   B) audacity   C) cowardice   D) meekness   E) modesty

3. To <u>remove</u> a stain
A) add   B) insert   C) attach   D) erase   E) affix

4. To <u>deny</u> the accusation
A) admit   B) accept   C) reject   D) confess   E) concede

5. To place an <u>emphasis</u> on quality
A) stress   B) ignore   C) disregard   D) overlook   E) forget

6. To <u>chisel</u> the wood
A) mend   B) repair   C) fix   D) restore   E) carve

7. To remain <u>inactive</u> for a long time
A) active   B) idle   C) energetic   D) lively   E) productive

8. To be <u>maudlin</u> after listening to music
A) unsentimental   B) rational   C) objective   D) sentimental   E) pragmatic

B. Sentence Completion – Missing Word

Select the correct answer from the options provided.

1. He spoke with a deep _____ for his childhood home, a place filled with cherished memories.
A) disdain   B) fondness   C) apathy   D) resentment

2. The tension in the room was _____, palpable to everyone present.
A) edgy   B) relaxing   C) calming   D) comfortable

3. Faced with an unexpected obstacle, they were forced to _____ and come up with a new plan.
A) improvise   B) mix up   C) jumble   D) disarrange

4. After running out of supplies, the robbers were forced to _____ to the police.
A) fight back   B) resist   C) persist   D) surrender

5. The scientists were careful to pack all the necessary _____ for their research expedition.
A) mementos   B) gifts   C) equipment   D) souvenirs

C. Homonyms

From the list below, fill in the blanks.

jam	scale	jamb	plane	rose	plain

1. Simple and without decoration   _____

2. The upright post at the side of a door or window   _____

3. To make smooth or even   _____

4. A device for weighing something or someone   _____

5. A prickly bush that bears fragrant flowers   _____

6. A level of existence, consciousness, or development   _____

7. Soar without moving the wings; glide   _____

8. A thick fruit preserve   _____

9. A pink or light red color   _____

10. A system of numerical values   _____

D. Analogies

Select the correct answer from the options provided.

1   POLLUTION is to ECOLOGICAL DAMAGE as
A) deforestation is to habitat loss
B) impartiality is to unfair advantage
C) propaganda is to ocean depletion
D) stasis is to traffic congestion
E) overfishing is to biased belief

2   JOVIAL is to MOROSE as
A) tranquil is to placid
B) cheerful is to downcast
C) wavering is to indecisive
D) discordant is to clashing
E) extravagant is to wasteful

3   LUCID is to CLEAR as
A) bubbly is to glum
B) outgoing is to withdrawn
C) merciful is to harsh
D) lively is to lifeless
E) murky is to obscure

4   DICTIONARY is to DEFINE as
A) page is to glue
B) thesaurus is to synonymize
C) record is to microphone
D) ditch is to shovel
E) brush is to painter

Set 26

A. Synonyms

Select the word that most closely matches the meaning of the word provided.

1. ISOLATE
A) join   B) separate   C) unite   D) combine   E) integrate

2. FAZE
A) calm   B) soothe   C) comfort   D) reassure   E) deter

3. VELOCITY
A) slowness   B) sluggishness C) speed   D) crawl   E) halt

4. SLUDGE
A) water   B) aqua   C) slush   D) clear   E) pure

5. CLARITY
A) obscurity   B) clearness   C) confusion   D) vagueness   E) complexity

6. OUTPUT
A) input   B) consumption   C) intake   D) production   E) expenditure

7. KINDLE
A) extinguish   B) ignite   C) douse   D) smother   E) snuff

8. PLUCK
A) push   B) thrust   C) shove   D) pull   E) propel

B. Sentence Completion - Double Blanks

Select the correct answer from the options provided.

1. He provided _____ and _____ details about the incident, leaving no room for doubt or interpretation.

A) vague...ambiguous   B) specific...precise   C) general...unspecific   D) irrelevant...unrelated

2. Knowing the volatile nature of the situation, she chose her words carefully, opting for a/an _____ approach to avoid _____.

A) aggressive...hostile   B) neutral...easy   C) diplomatic...conflict   D) fiery...provocative

3. His _____ leadership skills and unwavering determination guided the team through countless challenges to _____ their goals.

A) indecisive...hesitant   B) incompetent...ineffective   C) reckless...artless   D) capable...achieve

4. She put in great effort to _____ her home with colorful flowers, paintings, and other personal touches that reflected her _____ personality.

A) decorate...unique   B) renovate...modernize   C) tidy...organize   D) abandon...neglect

C. Antonyms

Pick the word that means the opposite or near opposite of the word provided.

1. ENNUI
A) excitement   B) tedium   C) apathy   D) lethargy   E) monotony

2. DISADVANTAGE
A) drawback   B) handicap   C) benefit   D) downside   E) obstacle

3. OCCURRENCE
A) event   B) happening   C) incident   D) absence   E) frequency

4. PERQUISITE
A) necessity   B) benefit   C) bonus   D) allowance   E) perk

5. IGNITE
A) light   B) burn   C) spark   D) extinguish   E) fire

6. TIMOROUS
A) bold   B) timid   C) shy   D) nervous   E) cowardly

7. RELATE
A) connect   B) associate   C) communicate   D) understand   E) alienate

8. SLIGHT
A) minor   B) significant   C) trivial   D) negligible   E) petty

D. Synonyms – Spelling

Complete the synonym of the word in **bold**.

1. **group**   cl__ st__ r

2. **runaway**   fu__ itiv__

3. **negotiate**   b__ rg__ in

4. **supplies**   p__ ovi__ ion__

5. **cower**   c__ ing__

6. **invalid**   in__ cce__ tab__ e

7. **proclamation**   de__ lar__ ti__ n

Set 27

A. Synonyms in context: Select the correct answer from the options provided.

1. To cause an earthquake
A) calm   B) tremor   C) stability   D) steadiness   E) tranquility

2. To query the database
A) answer   B) reply   C) question   D) acknowledge   E) confirm

3. To have the totality of evidence
A) part   B) fraction   C) segment   D) entirety   E) piece

4. To play with a formation on the field
A) arrangement   B) chaos   C) confusion   D) mess   E) disarray

5. To have a scraggly beard
A) neat   B) ragged   C) smooth   D) trim   E) sleek

6. To typify a genre
A) deviate   B) differ   C) diverge   D) vary   E) exemplify

7. To withhold the truth
A) reveal   B) disclose   C) expose   D) uncover   E) conceal

8. To entail considerable risk
A) exclude   B) omit   C) involve   D) disregard   E) ignore

B. Sentence Completion – Missing Word

Select the correct answer from the options provided.

1. He struggled to _____ his feelings for her, unsure of how she would react.
A) hide   B) repress   C) express   D) ignore

2. She sat faithfully _____ him, offering comfort and support during his time of need.
A) contrary   B) beside   C) above   D) behind

3. The speaker's voice was so _____ that it lulled the audience into a deep sleep.
A) energetic   B) enthralling   C) accelerating   D) soporific

4. The difference between the two objects was _____ almost imperceptible to the naked eye.
A) minuscule   B) significant   C) obvious   D) gigantic

5. Her _____ behavior was becoming increasingly difficult to tolerate.
A) agreeable   B) endearing   C) insufferable   D) tolerable

C. Homonyms

From the list below, fill in the blanks.

scene	date	seen	hall	clip	haul

1. The castle or house of a medieval king or noble   _____

2. To cause (something) to move by pulling or drawing   _____

3. One of the subdivisions of a play   _____

4. Past tense of "see"   _____

5. A device that holds or fastens something together   _____

6. A short segment of a film or video   _____

7. A particular day or point in time   _____

8. To transport in a vehicle   _____

9. The place or setting of an event   _____

10. A sweet, dark brown fruit with a single hard seed   _____

D. Analogies

Select the correct answer from the options provided.

1   PROGRAMMER is to CODE as
A)   gardener is to clippers
B)   builder is to blueprint
C)   writer is to words
D)   dancer is to choreography
E)   artist is to sketch

2   DESERT is to DRY as
A)   prairie is to rocky
B)   pure is to freshwater spring
C)   canyon is to flat
D)   rainforest is to humid
E)   glacier is to hike

3   OSTENTATIOUS is to MODEST as
A)   sturdy is to robust
B)   shrewd is to discerning
C)   secure is to firm
D)   significant is to impactful
E)   flashy is to understated

4   FLIMSY is to FRAIL as
A)   solid is to substantial
B)   haughty is to unassuming
C)   talkative is to quiet
D)   self-indulgent is to restrained
E)   flushed is to wan

Set 28

A. Synonyms

Select the word that most closely matches the meaning of the word provided.

1. OUTLAST
A) perish   B) die   C) succumb   D) survive   E) wither

2. RECOVER
A) worsen   B) heal   C) decline   D) relapse   E) regress

3. COMPILE
A) scatter   B) disperse   C) distribute   D) discard   E) collect

4. UNCONCERNED
A) concerned   B) interested   C) indifferent   D) caring   E) sympathetic

5. NUANCE
A) subtlety   B) clarity   C) plainness   D) simplicity   E) directness

6. IMMERSE
A) submerge   B) surface   C) rise   D) ascend   E) soar

7. EVAPORATE
A) condense   B) solidify   C) freeze   D) crystallize   E) vaporize

8. DELEGATE
A) retain   B) keep   C) assign   D) withhold   E) hoard

B. Sentence Completion - Double Blanks

Select the correct answer from the options provided.

1. His impulsive decision only served to _____ the situation, causing further _____ and resentment among the members of the group.

A) alleviate...resolve   B) clarify...explain   C) worsen...tension   D) ignore...disregard

2. He cast a _____ glance around the room, ensuring no one was _____ before making his move.

A) furtive...watching   B) direct...open   C) confident...proud   D) casual...unconcerned

3. The construction project caused major traffic_____, forcing motorists to _____ along unfamiliar routes.

A) proceed...continue   B) obstruct...block   C) disruptions...reroute   D) accelerate...speed up

4. The gang _____ a large sum of money from the businessman, threatening violence if he refused to _____ their demands.

A) demanded...fulfill   B) resist...defy   C) ignore...disregard   D) expose...reveal

C. Antonyms

Pick the word that means the opposite or near opposite of the word provided.

1. STRATEGIZE
A) plan   B) method   C) approach   D) improvise   E) policy

2. PRESENCE
A) absence   B) attendance   C) appearance   D) aura   E) company

3. BUMPY
A) belly   B) stomach   C) flat   D) abdomen   E) potbelly

4. BUZZ
A) silence   B) noise   C) rumor   D) excitement   E) vibration

5. PERSUADE
A) convince   B) influence   C) urge   D) induce   E) dissuade

6. GIBBERISH
A) absurdity   B) sense   C) folly   D) nonsense   E) prattle

7. SHUFFLE
A) shamble   B) stumble   C) limp   D) hobble   E) stride

8. PARTITION
A) union   B) separation   C) segment   D) wall   E) barrier

D. Synonyms – Spelling

Complete the synonym of the word in **bold**.

1. **jeopardize**   e__ dang__ r

2. **dumbstruck**   am__ ze__

3. **emit**   di__ char__ e

4. **conservation**   pr__ ser__ at__ on

5. **downsize**   d__ crea__ e

6. **quibble**   n__ tpi__ k

7. **feasible**   p__ ss__ ble

Set 29

A. Synonyms in context: Select the correct answer from the options provided.

1. To have a <u>uniformity</u> of style
A) consistency   B) variety   C) difference   D) contrast   E) discrepancy

2. To have a <u>depth</u> of knowledge
A) shallowness   B) triviality   C) simplicity   D) profundity   E) ignorance

3. To <u>exhale</u> the smoke
A) inhale   B) breathe out   C) swallow   D) gulp   E) suck

4. To <u>retire</u> from a job
A) join   B) start   C) begin   D) leave   E) initiate

5. To call a farmer a peasant is a <u>misnomer</u>
A) apt   B) misname   C) suitable   D) proper   E) accurate

6. To <u>dread</u> the exam
A) welcome   B) embrace   C) anticipate   D) fear   E) relish

7. To have a <u>scuffle</u> with an opponent
A) fight   B) harmony   C) agreement   D) accord   E) concord

8. To copy the speech <u>verbatim</u>
A) paraphrase   B) summarize   C) condense   D) abbreviate   E) literally

B. Sentence Completion – Missing Word
Select the correct answer from the options provided.

1. He _____ the role of leader without hesitation, stepping forward to guide the group.
A) relinquished   B) refused   C) avoided   D) assumed

2. The castle perched precariously on a/an _____ overlooking the vast valley below.
A) marsh   B) promontory   C) meadow   D) grassland

3. Wearing a uniform was _____, but most students chose to do so to show their school spirit.
A) mandatory   B) required   C) optional   D) encouraged

4. The author's vivid descriptions brought the _____ of the story to life.
A) summary   B) synopsis   C) outline   D) setting

5. The doctor was shocked by the patient's _____, showing no regard for the severity of their illness.
A) kindness   B) empathy   C) callousness   D) understanding

C. Homonyms

From the list below, fill in the blanks.

wait	deck	weight	cite	sight	site

1. To stay or remain in a place until a particular time or event _____

2. To quote or refer to someone or something as evidence _____

3. A floor or platform that extends from a building or a ship _____

4. A set of cards used for playing games _____

5. The amount that something weighs _____

6. The place where something is located or happens _____

7. To decorate or adorn something _____

8. A spectacle _____

9. To knock someone down with a punch _____

10. The process, power, or function of seeing _____

D. Analogies

Select the correct answer from the options provided.

1 DOGMATIC is to OPEN-MINDED as
A) bleak is to desolate
B) smelly is to gagging
C) stubborn is to flexible
D) frustrating is to irritating
E) idyllic is to dreamy

2 TANTALIZING is to TEMPTING as
A) biased is to impartial
B) inflexible is to dynamic
C) absolute is to multifaceted
D) arrogant is to considerate
E) repulsive is to revolting

3 THERMOMETER is to TEMPERATURE as
A) speedometer is to speed
B) altimeter is to heartbeat
C) stethoscope is to altitude
D) barometer is to earthquake
E) seismometer is to pressure

4 LEAF is to PLANT as
A) petal is to flower
B) stalk is to cornflake
C) wing is to larva
D) shark is to fin
E) anchor is to airship

Set 30

A. Synonyms

Select the word that most closely matches the meaning of the word provided.

1. APPAREL
A) emptiness   B) bareness   C) clothing   D) exposure   E) plainness

2. INDICATION
A) concealment   B) hiding   C) secrecy   D) sign   E) mystery

3. VALUE
A) worthlessness   B) worth   C) triviality   D) cheapness   E) futility

4. CONNOTATION
A) unchanging   B) diverse   C) matching   D) similar   E) implication

5. EXTREMITY
A) center   B) end   C) core   D) heart   E) essence

6. PLAGIARIZE
A) copy   B) create   C) invent   D) produce   E) compose

7. MAXIM
A) fact   B) reality   C) truth   D) certainty   E) proverb

8. STEEP
A) gentle   B) mild   C) gradual   D) sharp   E) level

B. Sentence Completion - Double Blanks
Select the correct answer from the options provided.

1. The police officer carefully _____ the scene of the crime, searching for any _____ that might lead to the perpetrator.

A) admired...appreciate   B) tainted...disrupt   C) dismissed...unnoticed D) inspected...clues

2. The lecture droned on, a monotonous stream of facts that left the students feeling both _____ and _____.

A) soothing...calm   B) dull...uninspired   C) vibrant...lively   D) colorful...tingling

3. He ate with a/an _____ appetite, _____ his meal in a matter of minutes and leaving no crumbs behind.

A) hesitant...reluctant   B) picky...selective   C) moderate...controlled D) voracious...devouring

4. Hundreds of people gathered in the streets to _____ against the government's policies, calling for _____ and social justice.

A) praise...endorse   B) protest...change   C) celebrate...honor   D) obey...submit

C. Antonyms

Pick the word that means the opposite or near opposite of the word provided.

1. GARRULOUS
A) talkative B) quiet C) chatty D) verbose E) wordy

2. AGGRESSOR
A) defender B) invader C) assailant D) bully E) antagonist

3. UNWISE
A) foolish B) imprudent C) silly D) reckless E) astute

4. QUEASY
A) nauseous B) sick C) uneasy D) dizzy E) healthy

5. DETRACTION
A) criticism B) praise C) disparagement D) defamation E) belittlement

6. SWELL
A) expand B) shrink C) inflate D) increase E) rise

7. BEGRUDGE
A) resent B) envy C) grudge D) appreciate E) covet

8. FOOLPROOF
A) fallible B) reliable C) flawless D) perfect E) fail-safe

D. Synonyms – Spelling

Complete the synonym of the word in **bold**.

1. **unrefined**   c__ud__

2. **movement**   mo__io__

3. **untoward**   im__rop__r

4. **vote**   b__llo__

5. **hold**   __lut__h

6. **stumble**   h__bb__e

7. **lunge**   t__rus__

Set 31

A. Synonyms in context: Select the correct answer from the options provided.

1. To have a <u>pastime</u> of reading
A) work   B) hobby   C) duty   D) task   E) chore

2. To be <u>unwieldy</u> in movements
A) graceful   B) agile   C) nimble   D) smooth   E) clumsy

3. To check the <u>initial</u> draft
A) final   B) last   C) ultimate   D) first   E) terminal

4. To be an <u>avid</u> learner
A) eager   B) apathetic   C) uninterested   D) bored   E) dispassionate

5. To <u>refine</u> the oil
A) contaminate   B) purify   C) taint   D) spoil   E) corrupt

6. To be <u>judicious</u> in decisions
A) foolish   B) silly   C) stupid   D) sensible   E) irrational

7. To <u>defuse</u> the situation
A) activate   B) resolve   C) explode   D) ignite   E) trigger

8. To be <u>opinionated</u> about everything
A) open-minded   B) flexible   C) intolerant   D) receptive   E) impartial

B. Sentence Completion – Missing Word

Select the correct answer from the options provided.

1. The crew of the ship staged a/an _____ against the captain, seizing control of the vessel.
A) celebration   B) party   C) gathering   D) mutiny

2. The teacher _____ him as the leader of the group project, recognizing his strong leadership skills.
A) appointed   B) vetoed   C) precluded   D) disregarded

3. They spent their days in _____ surroundings, surrounded by opulent furniture and rich fabrics.
A) simple   B) bare   C) modest   D) luxurious

4. After a wild night of partying, he woke up with a headache and a feeling of _____.
A) niceness   B) warmth   C) regret   D) fervor

5. Instead of pursuing their dreams, they chose to _____ and waste their lives away.
A) thrive   B) flourish   C) succeed   D) vegetate

C. Homonyms

From the list below, fill in the blanks.

roomer	shear	rumor	sheer	rock	fall

1. To cut off the fleece of a sheep   _____

2. A genre of popular music   _____

3. A person who rents a room in someone else's house   _____

4. Break off due to structural strain   _____

5. The solid mineral forming part of the surface of the earth   _____

6. Marked by great and continuous steepness   _____

7. A piece of gossip or unconfirmed information   _____

8. The season between Summer and Winter   _____

9. A decrease or decline in something   _____

10. Of very thin or transparent texture   _____

D. Analogies

Select the correct answer from the options provided.

1   SMOKING is to LUNG CANCER as
A) mosquito is to cataracts
B) sugar is to diabetes
C) obesity is to asthma
D) exercise is to cavities
E) fume is to fatigue

2   METICULOUS is to CAREFUL as
A) reckless is to haphazard
B) impulsive is to thoughtful
C) disrespectful is to respectful
D) stubborn is to open-minded
E) grumpy is to cheerful

3   IMPUDENT is to RESPECTFUL as
A) cursory is to superficial
B) thoughtless is to rash
C) rude is to polite
D) fragile is to vulnerable
E) naive is to gullible

4   SPINE is to BODY as
A) pipeline is to fluid
B) engine is to fast
C) boat is to keel
D) frame is to car
E) CPU is to wiring

Set 32

A. Synonyms

Select the word that most closely matches the meaning of the word provided.

1. ADMONISHMENT
A) reprimand   B) compliment   C) approval   D) commendation   E) reward

2. INVECTIVE
A) compliment   B) praise   C) flattery   D) admiration   E) criticism

3. HUSH
A) insider   B) silence   C) friend   D) ally   E) companion

4. OUTCAST
A) insider   B) member   C) friend   D) castaway   E) companion

5. TARNISHED
A) polished   B) stained   C) bright   D) enhanced   E) improved

6. IMPAIR
A) improve   B) enhance   C) repair   D) damage   E) heal

7. UNREASONABLE
A) reasonable   B) irrational   C) logical   D) sensible   E) sound

8. INTACT
A) broken   B) damaged   C) shattered   D) whole   E) torn

B. Sentence Completion - Double Blanks
Select the correct answer from the options provided.

1. The author used strong _____ devices throughout the _____, ensuring a smooth flow of ideas and arguments.

A) disruptive...chaotic   B) excessive...redundant   C) transitional...essay   D) contrary...varying

2. The old building was in a state of _____, but with careful planning and skilled workers, it was eventually _____ into a beautiful and functional space.

A) demolish...destroy   B) abandon...neglect   C) modernize...update   D) disrepair...renovated

3. Despite her illness, she radiated a remarkable _____ that_____ those around her.

A) energy...inspired   B) fragility...faintness   C) apathy...indifference D) morbidity...despair

4. The crime was so _____ that it sent _____ through the community, leaving everyone feeling violated and unsafe.

A) minor...trivial   B) heinous...shockwaves   C) justified...clear   D) ambiguous...unclear

C. Antonyms

Pick the word that means the opposite or near opposite of the word provided.

1. ROBUST
A) strong   B) frail   C) vigorous   D) solid   E) healthy

2. OVERBEARING
A) domineering   B) submissive   C) arrogant   D) oppressive   E) controlling

3. BRIBERY
A) honesty   B) inducement   C) pay-off   D) graft   E) influence

4. DISBAND
A) dissolve   B) disperse   C) scatter   D) break up   E) assemble

5. IMPASSIONED
A) passionate   B) impassive   C) ardent   D) enthusiastic   E) zealous

6. HYPE
A) excitement   B) calm   C) fuss   D) commotion   E) fanfare

7. GAZE
A) save   B) glance   C) recover   D) reinstate   E) compensate

8. RACKET
A) noise   B) peace   C) din   D) row   E) uproar

D. Synonyms – Spelling

Complete the synonym of the word in **bold**.

1. **extinguish**   q__en__h

2. **straits**   d__ffi__ult__

3. **heroism**   b__ave__y

4. **stultified**   bo__e__

5. **tool**   i__st__um__nt

6. **marginal**   __lig__t

7. **overwhelm**   ov__rp__wer

Set 33

A. Synonyms in context: Select the correct answer from the options provided.

1. To have a semblance of authority
A) reality   B) appearance   C) fact   D) substance   E) essence

2. To have a cadence in music
A) silence   B) stillness   C) agreement   D) peace   E) rhythm

3. To have nervousness before an interview
A) calmness   B) anxiety   C) assurance   D) composure   E) tranquility

4. To have an accurate projection of the future
A) hindsight   B) past   C) forecast   D) memory   E) recall

5. To be curative in methods
A) harmful   B) damaging   C) injurious   D) healing   E) destructive

6. To equate two values
A) differ   B) equal   C) vary   D) diverge   E) distinguish

7. To retort an insult
A) reply   B) query   C) inquiry   D) request   E) appeal

8. To have a keenness for adventure
A) apathy   B) indifference   C) boredom   D) enthusiasm   E) lethargy

B. Sentence Completion – Missing Word

Select the correct answer from the options provided.

1. The teacher gave him a/an _____ nod, acknowledging his correct answer.
A) disapproving   B) approving   C) indifferent   D) critical

2. The musician experimented with different _____ of the traditional melody, creating a unique and modern interpretation.
A) variations   B) fakes   C) molds   D) archetypes

3. The archaeological _____ revealed fascinating artifacts from a bygone era.
A) dump   B) site   C) deposit   D) scrapyard

4. They waited patiently, the _____ between each chime of the clock seeming an eternity.
A) figures   B) numbers   C) interval   D) ciphers

5. The once sweet friendship turned unpleasant, filled with sourness and _____ .
A) laughter   B) joy   C) harmony   D) bitterness

C. Homonyms

From the list below, fill in the blanks.

ring	genes	rowed	jeans	road	rode

1. A specific sequence of nucleotides in DNA or RNA   _____

2. A type of trousers made from denim   _____

3. A surface covered with asphalt for vehicles to travel on   _____

4. Propelled by means of oars   _____

5. Past tense of "ride"   _____

6. A route or way to an end, conclusion, or circumstance   _____

7. A small band, typically of precious metal   _____

8. A circular object, shape, or arrangement   _____

9. A group of people having a common feature or purpose   _____

10. A loud resonant sound made by a bell or a telephone   _____

D. Analogies

Select the correct answer from the options provided.

1   HAND is to CLOCK as
A) nose is to smell
B) needle is to syringe
C) bottle is to mouth
D) pedal is to speed
E) string is to guitarist

2   VERBOSE is to WORDY as
A) playful is to light
B) mature is to child
C) impulsive is to cautious
D) conventional is to trade
E) concise is to succinct

3   FIRE is to ASHES as
A) ski is to snow
B) shade is to winter
C) soil is to seed
D) wound is to scar
E) warmth is to sun

4   PRAGMATIC is to DREAMY as
A) practical is to idealistic
B) intricate is to complicated
C) extensive is to lengthy
D) clear is to transparent
E) direct is to straight

Set 34

A. Synonyms

Select the word that most closely matches the meaning of the word provided.

1. OUTLIVE
A) die   B) perish   C) survive   D) succumb   E) wither

2. PERJURE
A) lie   B) swear   C) affirm   D) confirm   E) verify

3. EMBOLDEN
A) discourage   B) deter   C) dissuade   D) encourage   E) inhibit

4. DEPRESSING
A) cheerful   B) mournful   C) happy   D) lively   E) radiant

5. FURY
A) calmness   B) rage   C) peace   D) tranquility   E) harmony

6. DEEM
A) disregard   B) ignore   C) consider   D) overlook   E) dismiss

7. UNDERMINE
A) strengthen   B) support   C) reinforce   D) enhance   E) weaken

8. CONCUR
A) disagree   B) agree   C) oppose   D) dispute   E) object

B. Sentence Completion - Double Blanks
Select the correct answer from the options provided.

1. The manager imposed _____ restrictions on his employees, creating an _____ of fear and resentment.

A) undue...environment   B) beneficial...necessary   C) helpful...supportive   D) appropriate...fair

2. As she crossed the finish line, she was overcome with _____ at having achieved her _____.

A) regret...resignation   B) elation...goal   C) anxiety...apprehension   D) exhaustion...fatigue

3. The secret message was carefully _____ into a harmless-looking document, ensuring it would remain _____ from prying eyes.

A) delete...destroy   B) decipher...decode   C) encoded...hidden   D) translate...clarify

4. The customer service representative was friendly and _____ to my inquiries, providing _____ information and resolving my issue promptly.

A) unfeeling...impassive   B) aggressive...hostile   C) unhelpful...dismissive   D) responsive...helpful

C. Antonyms

Pick the word that means the opposite or near opposite of the word provided.

1. SURREAL
A) unreal B) realistic C) dreamlike D) strange E) fantastic

2. DEPART
A) leave B) go C) exit D) quit E) arrive

3. SUBORDINATE
A) inferior B) boss C) junior D) dependent E) secondary

4. METHOD
A) technique B) manner C) guesswork D) style E) science

5. INTEGRAL
A) optional B) vital C) important D) fundamental E) necessary

6. DISILLUSION
A) disappoint B) disabuse C) disenchant D) enchant E) dissatisfy

7. AMENABLE
A) agreeable B) cooperative C) stubborn D) willing E) obedient

8. INHIBIT
A) restrain B) hinder C) motivate D) prevent E) impede

D. Synonyms – Spelling

Complete the synonym of the word in **bold**.

1. **impulse**   i__stin__t

2. **zealot**   __an__tic

3. **manager**   su__ervi__or

4. **exude**   re__ea__e

5. **impel**   c__mp__l

6. **empower**   a__th__ri__e

7. **spear**   ja__el__n

Set 35

A. Synonyms in context: Select the correct answer from the options provided.

1. To be <u>unrelenting</u> in pursuit
A) relentless   B) yielding   C) flexible   D) merciful   E) compassionate

2. To <u>imprint</u> name on paper
A) erase   B) remove   C) delete   D) wipe   E) stamp

3. To have a <u>consensus</u> with the team
A) disagreement   B) agreement   C) dispute   D) argument   E) dissent

4. To be <u>sassy</u> in remarks
A) respectful   B) polite   C) courteous   D) deferential   E) cheeky

5. To have <u>indestructible</u> armor
A) destructible   B) invincible   C) fragile   D) weak   E) breakable

6. To be <u>heterogeneous</u> in composition
A) homogeneous   B) uniform   C) diverse   D) identical   E) same

7. To be in a <u>surly</u> mood
A) pleasant   B) friendly   C) polite   D) courteous   E) rude

8. To be <u>overzealous</u> in work
A) overenthusiastic   B) apathetic   C) moderate   D) balanced   E) reasonable

B. Sentence Completion – Missing Word

Select the correct answer from the options provided.

1. She was the _____ of grace, her every movement elegant and refined.
A) epitome   B) misrepresentation   C) parody   D) perversion

2. The town on the outskirts was known for its _____ atmosphere, a stark contrast to the bustling city life.
A) exciting   B) fast-paced   C) staid   D) energetic

3. The city erupted in a/an _____ of joy as the news of the victory spread.
A) murmur   B) outburst   C) sigh   D) whisper

4. He _____ through the airport, anxious to catch his flight.
A) walked   B) strolled   C) sauntered   D) rushed

5. The scientist's _____ into the behavior of the virus led to a breakthrough in the research.
A) ignorance   B) insight   C) blindness   D) confusion

C. Homonyms

From the list below, fill in the blanks.

pedal	peddle	hoard	horde	right	point

1. A temporary board fence put around a building   _____

2. To sell something, especially on the streets   _____

3. A supply or fund stored up and often hidden away   _____

4. A moral or legal entitlement to have or do something _____

5. A sharp or tapered end of something   _____

6. A lever operated by the foot   _____

7. To ride a bicycle   _____

8. To do something correctly   _____

9. A large group of people or animals   _____

10. A dot or other punctuation mark, especially a period _____

D. Analogies

Select the correct answer from the options provided.

1   JOLLY is to GRIM as
A) gruff is to rude
B) affable is to cordial
C) bright is to dim
D) churlish is to unfriendly
E) genial is to kind

2   CONVIVIAL is to FRIENDLY as
A) impolite is to hostile
B) jubilant is to miserable
C) vivid is to faded
D) gleeful is to melancholy
E) sparkling is to dull

3   DOCTOR is to STETHOSCOPE as
A) musician is to song
B) carpenter is to saw
C) teacher is to pupil
D) brush is to painter
E) chef is to waiter

4   MONDAY is to TUESDAY as
A) wednesday is to friday
B) sunday is to saturday
C) december is to march
D) january is to february
E) july is to september

Set 36

A. Synonyms

Select the word that most closely matches the meaning of the word provided.

1. MULISH
A) flexible   B) compliant   C) obedient   D) docile   E) stubborn

2. GRASP
A) understand   B) confuse   C) misinterpret   D) obscure   E) complicate

3. MORBID
A) cheerful   B) gloomy   C) happy   D) lively   E) radiant

4. ELABORATE
A) simple   B) detailed   C) brief   D) concise   E) vague

5. BLINK
A) stare   B) gaze   C) glare   D) peer   E) wink

6. SANCTUARY
A) danger   B) refuge   C) peril   D) risk   E) harm

7. IMPECCABLE
A) flawless   B) flawed   C) faulty   D) defective   E) erroneous

8. ABIDE
A) disobey   B) defy   C) obey   D) rebel   E) ignore

B. Sentence Completion - Double Blanks
Select the correct answer from the options provided.

1. The victor couldn't resist to _____ over his opponent's _____, further humiliating him in front of the crowd.

A) apologize...regret   B) respect...admire   C) gloat...defeat   D) console...sympathize

2. The doctor warned against the _____ surgery, citing the potential for _____ and long-term recovery time.

A) routine...minor   B) invasive...complications   C) beneficial...essential   D) simple...straightforward

3. The morning dew _____ on the grass like a million tiny diamonds, creating a _____ spectacle.

A) glistened...breathtaking   B) faded...disappear   C) rotten...decay   D) freeze...solidify

4. The thought of her own _____ suddenly became a stark reality, prompting her to_____ on her life and make changes.

A) immortality...eternity   B) youth...everlasting   C) mortality...reflect   D) strength...unshakeable

C. Antonyms

Pick the word that means the opposite or near opposite of the word provided.

1. BLATANT
A) obvious   B) flagrant   C) loud   D) glaring   E) subtle

2. ABDUCT
A) kidnap   B) capture   C) release   D) snatch   E) hijack

3. OFFENCE
A) fault   B) virtue   C) sin   D) crime   E) misdemeanor

4. DEPRECATE
A) criticize   B) belittle   C) condemn   D) approve   E) denounce

5. IRRESOLUTE
A) indecisive   B) decisive   C) uncertain   D) doubtful   E) wavering

6. HYSTERIA
A) calmness   B) frenzy   C) madness   D) mania   E) craze

7. DISPLAY
A) show   B) exhibit   C) demonstrate   D) present   E) hide

8. DEFIANCE
A) resistance   B) obedience   C) challenge   D) opposition   E) disobedience

D. Synonyms – Spelling

Complete the synonym of the word in **bold**.

1. **alteration**   v__riat__on

2. **skeptical**   do__bt__ul

3. **tedious**   ti__eso__e

4. **sovereign**   __upr__me

5. **dearth**   sc__rc__ty

6. **preoccupied**   __ist__ac__ed

7. **muddy**   m__rk__

Set 37

A. Synonyms in context: Select the correct answer from the options provided.

1. To <u>unravel</u> a mystery
A) complicate   B) confuse   C) obscure   D) perplex   E) solve

2. To experience <u>enjoyment</u> in life
A) pleasure   B) pain   C) suffering   D) misery   E) sorrow

3. To have a <u>generality</u> of knowledge
A) specificity   B) overview   C) precision   D) accuracy   E) exactness

4. To perform a <u>soliloquy</u> in a play
A) dialogue   B) conversation   C) discussion   D) monologue   E) communication

5. To be <u>aberrant</u> in behavior
A) abnormal   B) usual   C) regular   D) standard   E) typical

6. To <u>unearth</u> a treasure
A) bury   B) hide   C) conceal   D) discover   E) obscure

7. To be known for <u>philanthropy</u> for the poor
A) greed   B) selfishness   C) charity   D) miserliness   E) meanness

8. To have a <u>tinge</u> of regret
A) abundance   B) plenty   C) excess   D) surplus   E) hint

B. Sentence Completion – Missing Word
Select the correct answer from the options provided.

1. The sudden spin made her feel _____ and disoriented.
A) calm   B) stable   C) focused   D) dizzy

2. He _____ between two choices, unsure of which path to take.
A) firmly   B) committed   C) vacillated   D) persisted

3. Her hand _____ as she signed the important document.
A) trembled   B) confident   C) tremulous   D) composed

4. He had a/an _____ attitude towards his work, showing little enthusiasm or motivation.
A) energetic   B) diligent   C) dedicated   D) lackadaisical

5. The _____ slithered through the undergrowth, hidden from view.
A) reptile   B) dog   C) bird   D) fish

C. Homonyms

From the list below, fill in the blanks.

role	roll	fine	bark	note	barque

1.   To move something by turning it over and over   _____

2.   The rough outer covering of a tree   _____

3.   A character assigned or assumed   _____

4.   To notice or pay attention to something   _____

5.   A scroll   _____

6.   A sum of money that is imposed as a penalty   _____

7.   A part played by an actor or singer   _____

8.   A sailing ship with three masts   _____

9.   To record or write down something   _____

10.   Well or healthy   _____

D. Analogies

Select the correct answer from the options provided.

1   EXPRESSIVE is to ARTICULATE as
A)   mundane is to thrilling
B)   spotless is to shabby
C)   collected is to flustered
D)   inarticulate is to tongue-tied
E)   easygoing is to demanding

2   ABUNDANT is to SCARCITY as
A)   plentiful is to rare
B)   magnificent is to splendid
C)   terrible is to awful
D)   selfish is to greedy
E)   indifferent is to apathetic

3   VERSE is to POEM as
A)   feeling is to story
B)   chord is to painting
C)   chip is to masterpiece
D)   thread is to tapestry
E)   scene is to play

4   WATER is to BOIL as
A)   cough is to illness
B)   sapling is to tree
C)   ice is to melt
D)   melody is to whistle
E)   blaze is to flicker

Set 38

A. Synonyms

Select the word that most closely matches the meaning of the word provided.

1. RESTLESS
A) uneasy   B) serene   C) peaceful   D) tranquil   E) relaxed

2. VULNERABILITY
A) strength   B) power   C) resilience   D) fortitude   E) weakness

3. EVOKE
A) suppress   B) elicit   C) inhibit   D) repress   E) silence

4. INNATE
A) natural   B) learned   C) artificial   D) cultivated   E) extrinsic

5. SNARE
A) release   B) free   C) trap   D) rescue   E) save

6. PSYCHOLOGY
A) art   B) behaviorism   C) music   D) poetry   E) painting

7. RECUPERATE
A) worsen   B) deteriorate   C) decline   D) recover   E) regress

8. PETITION
A) request   B) order   C) demand   D) dictate   E) impose

B. Sentence Completion - Double Blanks

Select the correct answer from the options provided.

1. I absolutely _____ violence in any form and believe that all _____ should be resolved peacefully.

A) ignore...disregard   B) condone...justify   C) embrace...endorse   D) abhor...conflicts

2. After months of saving, she finally had enough money to _____ the dress of her _____.

A) abandon...discard   B) purchase...dreams   C) return...refund   D) admire...long for

3. My top _____ is to ensure the _____ and well-being of my family. Everything else comes second.

A) hassle...burden   B) desire...want   C) priority...safety   D) distraction...diversion

4. He struggled to find the right _____ to express his feelings, fumbling over his words and failing to _____ the intended message.

A) phrase...convey   B) mumble...incoherently   C) shout...aggressively   D) whisper...secretly

C. Antonyms

Pick the word that means the opposite or near opposite of the word provided.

1. APOLOGETIC
A) sorry   B) unrepentant   C) remorseful   D) repentant   E) contrite

2. GROOVE
A) channel   B) furrow   C) ridge   D) slot   E) track

3. IDOL
A) hero   B) star   C) icon   D) enemy   E) protagonist

4. OUTLANDISH
A) strange   B) bizarre   C) ordinary   D) eccentric   E) exotic

5. RESTORE
A) repair   B) damage   C) recover   D) revive   E) return

6. RATTY
A) shabby   B) irritable   C) ragged   D) cranky   E) pleasant

7. EMERGE
A) occur   B) disappear   C) transpire   D) befall   E) ensue

8. GIDDY
A) dizzy   B) frivolous   C) serious   D) silly   E) vertiginous

D. Synonyms – Spelling

Complete the synonym of the word in **bold**.

1. **utter**   ex__re__s

2. **orient**   po__iti__n

3. **disease**   __ilm__nt

4. **questionable**   d__ba__a__le

5. **customary**   re__ula__

6. **widespread**   __re__al__nt

7. **predicament**   di__em__a

Set 39

A. Synonyms in context: Select the correct answer from the options provided.

1. To <u>demonstrate</u> a skill
A) hide   B) conceal   C) obscure   D) mask   E) show

2. To have an <u>exuberant</u> personality
A) joyful   B) dull   C) tedious   D) monotonous   E) dreary

3. To <u>scorn</u> technological advances
A) respect   B) admiration   C) esteem   D) honor   E) contempt

4. To <u>stifle</u> the laughter
A) release   B) suppress   C) vent   D) unleash   E) liberate

5. To <u>intercept</u> the pass
A) miss   B) drop   C) lose   D) fail   E) catch

6. To have a <u>carefree</u> attitude
A) worried   B) relaxed   C) nervous   D) stressed   E) tense

7. To be <u>ravenous</u> after fasting
A) full   B) satisfied   C) satiated   D) stuffed   E) hungry

8. To <u>polarize</u> the audience
A) unite   B) divide   C) connect   D) link   E) merge

B. Sentence Completion – Missing Word

Select the correct answer from the options provided.

1. The stranger approached us with a/an _____ look on his face, raising suspicions.
A) friendly   B) welcoming   C) belligerent   D) agreeable

2. Despite facing hardship, she showed remarkable _____, never giving up hope.
A) weakness   B) cowardice   C) fragility   D) fortitude

3. He spoke with a/an _____ tongue, easily manipulating others with his smooth words.
A) glib   B) awkward   C) stuttering   D) hesitant

4. He decided to _____ the negative comments from his memory, focusing on the positive instead.
A) recall   B) expunge   C) remember   D) dwell on

5. The family _____ a complaint with the management about the poor service.
A) accepted   B) praised   C) ignored   D) lodged

C. Homonyms

From the list below, fill in the blanks.

plum	hoarse	horse	plumb	net	mean

1. A large, domesticated animal _____

2. Rough or harsh sounding _____

3. To have or indicate a particular meaning or intention _____

4. An interconnected system or group _____

5. A weight attached to a line to indicate a vertical direction _____

6. Unkind, spiteful, or unfair _____

7. To intend or plan to do something _____

8. The amount remaining after deductions are made _____

9. A small, round, purple fruit _____

10. A fabric made of threads or cords that are woven together _____

D. Analogies

Select the correct answer from the options provided.

1   SPOON is to EATING as
A)   moon is to night
B)   eating is to food
C)   hammering is to nailing
D)   shoveling is to digging
E)   knife is to slicing

2   HONEY is to SWEET as
A)   fish is to boat
B)   movie is to film
C)   hot is to fire
D)   pepper is to spicy
E)   cold is to snow

3   INVOLUNTARY is to VOLUNTARY as
A)   learn is to study
B)   deny is to lie
C)   forced is to chosen
D)   retreat is to regress
E)   negate is to reject

4   AWAIT is to ANTICIPATE as
A)   casual is to official
B)   expect is to foresee
C)   partial is to whole
D)   idle is to busy
E)   hidden is to seen

Set 40

A. Synonyms

Select the word that most closely matches the meaning of the word provided.

1. NONCHALANT
A) formal
B) casual
C) earnest
D) attentive
E) concerned

2. NOXIOUSNESS
A) benignity
B) harmlessness
C) mildness
D) safety
E) toxicity

3. OASIS
A) haven
B) wasteland
C) wilderness
D) barrenness
E) dryness

4. DEFLECT
A) attract
B) divert
C) lure
D) magnetize
E) entice

5. GRANDEUR
A) plainness
B) splendor
C) modesty
D) mediocrity
E) dullness

6. CONCEIVE
A) forget
B) ignore
C) neglect
D) overlook
E) imagine

7. EXIT
A) leave
B) arrive
C) come
D) join
E) stay

8. EARSHOT
A) silence
B) quietness
C) hearing
D) deafness
E) noiselessness

B. Sentence Completion - Double Blanks
Select the correct answer from the options provided.

1. The instructions were so _____ that it was nearly _____ to understand what was required, leading to confusion and frustration.

A) precise...clear   B) imprecise...impossible   C) detailed...complete   D) concise...brief

2. The detective gathered enough evidence to reach a _____ about the case, leaving no room for doubt about the perpetrator's _____.

A) uncertain...inexact   B) lacking...unclear   C) shy...hesitant   D) conclusion...identity

3. He served a brief _____ in the military, gaining _____ experience and skills that would later benefit him in his civilian life.

A) hiatus...break   B) stint...valuable   C) increase...extension   D) dismissal...discharge

4. The _____ suitcase was difficult to handle and _____, making travel a cumbersome and tiring experience.

A) sleek...streamlined   B) light...portable   C) bulky...maneuver   D) compact...efficient

C. Antonyms

Pick the word that means the opposite or near opposite of the word provided.

1. FIRST
A) neat   B) stylish   C) smart   D) last   E) trim

2. ABNORMALITY
A) occurrence   B) normality   C) marvel   D) wonder   E) spectacle

3. ENMITY
A) hostility   B) hatred   C) animosity   D) antagonism   E) friendship

4. INTRODUCE
A) present   B) conclude   C) launch   D) initiate   E) acquaint

5. REASSESSMENT
A) evaluation   B) review   C) revision   D) confirmation   E) reevaluation

6. ENDURABLE
A) bearable   B) intolerable   C) manageable   D) livable   E) sufferable

7. MERCANTILE
A) noncommercial   B) trade   C) business   D) market   E) economic

8. DISPOSE
A) discard   B) throw away   C) hoard   D) dump   E) eliminate

D. Synonyms – Spelling

Complete the synonym of the word in **bold**.

1. **reflective**   t__oug__tf__l

2. **tacky**   s__od__y

3. **tolerable**   be__ra__le

4. **hypothesis**   __he__ry

5. **mention**   al__ud__

6. **borderline**   ma__gi__al

7. **afraid**   ter__if__ed

Set 41

A. Synonyms in context: Select the correct answer from the options provided.

1. To have <u>trauma</u> from an accident
A) healing   B) recovery   C) cure   D) distress   E) therapy

2. To <u>culminate</u> the speech with a joke
A) begin   B) end   C) injury   D) commence   E) launch

3. To have an <u>underlying</u> condition
A) obvious   B) evident   C) clear   D) apparent   E) hidden

4. To <u>bore</u> the listeners
A) tire   B) fascinate   C) captivate   D) intrigue   E) entertain

5. To <u>argue</u> with the boss
A) agree   B) concur   C) consent   D) accept   E) dispute

6. To have an <u>uneven</u> surface
A) irregular   B) regular   C) consistent   D) steady   E) uniform

7. To see a <u>silhouette</u> in the dark
A) detail   B) feature   C) aspect   D) outline   E) trait

8. To be <u>elated</u> by a news
A) depressed   B) happy   C) miserable   D) gloomy   E) unhappy

B. Sentence Completion – Missing Word

Select the correct answer from the options provided.

1. He fought back with _____ determination, refusing to give up despite the obstacles.
A) weak   B) hesitant   C) persistent   D) faltering

2. Access to clean water is _____ for human survival.
A) unnecessary   B) essential   C) optional   D) disposable

3. The doctor prescribed a new _____ to help alleviate the patient's symptoms.
A) disease   B) affliction   C) symptom   D) remedy

4. The horses provided the only _____ across the vast plains of Magnolia.
A) conveyance   B) accommodation   C) shelter   D) home

5. The prisoner languished in a dark and damp _____, isolated from the outside world.
A) dungeon   B) palace   C) mansion   D) villa

C. Homonyms

From the list below, fill in the blanks.

sum	some	stationary	match	stationery	light

1. Being one, a part, or an unspecified number of something   _____

2. Fixed in a station, course, or mode   _____

3. A contest in which people or teams compete   _____

4. A particular amount of money   _____

5. A source of illumination or guidance   _____

6. Materials (such as paper, pens, and ink) for writing   _____

7. Not moving or changing position   _____

8. A person or thing that is similar to or harmonizes with another   _____

9. Having a relatively low weight or density   _____

10. The whole amount or the aggregate   _____

D. Analogies

Select the correct answer from the options provided.

1   OPALESCENT is to DULL as
A) innovative is to creative
B) honest is to truthful
C) stingy is to hoarding
D) quiet is to silent
E) colorful is to drab

2   PEDANTIC is to NITPICKING as
A) bright is to dark
B) casual is to laid-back
C) vivid is to pale
D) spectrum is to color
E) flowery is to simple

3   LANGUAGE is to ENGLISH as
A) punk is to genre
B) crimson is to shade
C) instrument is to guitar
D) breed is to dog
E) futsal is to game

4   FARMER is to PLOW as
A) miner is to pickaxe
B) loom is to weaver
C) multimeter is to electrician
D) wheel is to potter
E) score is to composer

Set 42

A. Synonyms

Select the word that most closely matches the meaning of the word provided.

1. GENEALOGY
A) future   B) ancestry   C) possibility   D) potential   E) expectation

2. BIOGRAPHY
A) fiction   B) life story   C) invention   D) fabrication   E) falsehood

3. PUPPETEER
A) puppet   B) follower   C) subordinate   D) dependent   E) manipulator

4. ROAM
A) settle   B) wander   C) remain   D) rest   E) linger

5. CREASE
A) unfold   B) smooth   C) flatten   D) straighten   E) fold

6. YELP
A) laugh   B) cry   C) chuckle   D) grin   E) smile

7. ADHERENT
A) leader   B) guide   C) master   D) mentor   E) follower

8. INDELIBLE
A) erasable   B) permanent   C) temporary   D) fading   E) transient

B. Sentence Completion - Double Blanks

Select the correct answer from the options provided.

1. He felt a deep sense of _____ when he realized his mistake, _____ by his own careless actions.

A) pride...approval   B) pursuit...acting   C) district...peaceful   D) shame...embarrassed

2. He completely _____ the job, leaving a_____ in his wake and forcing others to clean up after his mistakes.

A) botched...mess   B) improved...enhance   C) completed...finish   D) started...initiate

3. Everyone makes _____; the important thing is to _____ from them and not repeat them.

A) statements...remarks   B) successes...feats   C) mistakes...learn   D) decisions...choices

4. The workmanship was _____ at best, with _____ flaws and shortcuts taken throughout the project.

A) exciting...notable   B) particular...precise   C) excellent...superior   D) shoddy...visible

C. Antonyms

Pick the word that means the opposite or near opposite of the word provided.

1. WAIT
A) delay   B) pause   C) hurry   D) hesitate   E) postpone

2. HAGGARD
A) fresh   B) weary   C) worn   D) exhausted   E) pale

3. PIGMENT
A) color   B) dye   C) hue   D) colorless   E) shade

4. DOWNCAST
A) depressed   B) sad   C) positive   D) dejected   E) despondent

5. PREVALENT
A) common   B) rare   C) frequent   D) dominant   E) popular

6. SLY
A) cunning   B) honest   C) sneaky   D) wily   E) foxy

7. EXEMPT
A) liable   B) excused   C) spared   D) immune   E) excepted

8. ENCOUNTER
A) meet   B) face   C) avoid   D) experience   E) bump into

D. Synonyms – Spelling

Complete the synonym of the word in **bold**.

1. **ordain**   __pp__int

2. **suspension**   ex__lusi__n

3. **lambaste**   cr__tic__ze

4. **quench**   s__ti__fy

5. **govern**   co__tr__l

6. **component**   el__me__t

7. **fade**   di__ap__e__r

Set 43

A. Synonyms in context: Select the correct answer from the options provided.

1. To be <u>slovenly</u> in appearance
A) neat   B) sloppy   C) clean   D) orderly   E) immaculate

2. To have a <u>warehouse</u> for goods
A) empty   B) vacant   C) bare   D) storehouse   E) hollow

3. To be an <u>egotist</u> in behavior
A) narcissist   B) selfless   C) generous   D) kind   E) benevolent

4. To have a <u>hawkish</u> policy
A) dovish   B) peaceful   C) pacifist   D) conciliatory   E) aggressive

5. To <u>confuse</u> the students
A) enlighten   B) clarify   C) perplex   D) inform   E) instruct

6. To <u>enchant</u> with a smile
A) repel   B) charm   C) offend   D) annoy   E) irritate

7. To <u>scrawl</u> a name on a paper
A) print   B) stamp   C) imprint   D) engrave   E) scribble

8. To <u>jettison</u> the extra weight
A) keep   B) retain   C) preserve   D) maintain   E) discard

B. Sentence Completion – Missing Word
Select the correct answer from the options provided.

1. The repeated information was _____ and only served to confuse the audience.
A) redundant   B) useful   C) necessary   D) informative

2. He made a valiant _____ to rescue the child from the burning building.
A) attempt   B) retreat   C) escape   D) abandonment

3. The rules were strict and _____ any deviation from the established procedures.
A) encouraged   B) permitted   C) disallowed   D) sanctioned

4. The town lay in a/an _____ state, ravaged by disease and famine.
A) thriving   B) prosperous   C) flourishing   D) moribund

5. The salesman used his _____ charm to convince the customer to buy the product.
A) unrefined   B) slick   C) rough   D) blunt

C. Homonyms

From the list below, fill in the blanks.

letter	mousse	not	naught	knot	moose

1. Another word for "nothing" _____

2. A light spongy food usually containing cream or gelatin _____

3. A foamy preparation used in styling hair _____

4. A large, antlered mammal _____

5. An adverb meaning "no" _____

6. A tie or loop in a rope or cord _____

7. A written, typed, or printed communication _____

8. A symbol constituting a unit of an alphabet _____

9. A measure of the speed of ships and aircraft _____

10. The initial of a school awarded to a student for achievement _____

D. Analogies

Select the correct answer from the options provided.

1   EXERCISE is to HEALTH as
A) hydration is to water
B) reading is to mind
C) centering is to speaking
D) security is to saving
E) refinement is to repetition

2   SHUSH is to SHOUT as
A) convict is to burden
B) ostracize is to alienate
C) ridicule is to belittle
D) silence is to noise
E) accuse is to incriminate

3   VINDICATE is to CLEAR as
A) directness is to deflection
B) curiosity is to ambiguity
C) clarity is to obfuscation
D) measurement is to estimation
E) condemn is to censure

4   FLASHLIGHT is to ILLUMINATING as
A) translator is to interpreting
B) exploring is to telescope
C) guiding is to map
D) microphone is to deciphering
E) dictionary is to amplifying

Set 44

A. Synonyms

Select the word that most closely matches the meaning of the word provided.

1. UNISON
A) discord   B) dissonance   C) conflict   D) harmony   E) disagreement

2. UNSTOPPABLE
A) persistent   B) halting   C) hesitant   D) timid   E) fearful

3. FUSE
A) separate   B) divide   C) split   D) part   E) join

4. REFRESH
A) stale   B) renew   C) outdated   D) obsolete   E) worn-out

5. EXACT
A) precise   B) unclear   C) ambiguous   D) fuzzy   E) imprecise

6. LIGHTHEARTED
A) gloomy   B) sad   C) carefree   D) miserable   E) sorrowful

7. CAREFULNESS
A) recklessness   B) caution   C) rashness   D) imprudence   E) indiscretion

8. IMPROVE
A) worsen   B) deteriorate   C) impair   D) degrade   E) enhance

B. Sentence Completion - Double Blanks

Select the correct answer from the options provided.

1. His _____ disregard for the rules and regulations only served to _____ his authority and credibility.

A) flagrant...undermine   B) subtle...discreet   C) civil...admirable   D) tame...compliant

2. The politician's inflammatory words only served to _____ the already divided community, driving a deeper wedge between _____ factions.

A) unite...cohesively   B) soothe...calm   C) understand...empathize   D) wedge...opposing

3. He spoke in veiled _____ , leaving his true _____ ambiguous and open to interpretation.

A) insinuations...intentions   B) statements...details   C) ease...honesty   D) flatters...fawning

4. She was a scholar of the highest _____ and her contributions to the field were _____ and respected by all.

A) poorness...average   B) caliber...recognized   C) inability...futility   D) obscurity...triviality

C. Antonyms

Pick the word that means the opposite or near opposite of the word provided.

1. EXCLUDE
A) include   B) bar   C) omit   D) ban   E) eliminate

2. DEMISE
A) death   B) end   C) downfall   D) birth   E) collapse

3. FACTION
A) offshoot   B) group   C) cluster   D) circle   E) solo

4. REVEAL
A) tag   B) conceal   C) mark   D) identify   E) classify

5. DECREASE
A) surge   B) lower   C) diminish   D) decline   E) lessen

6. SALUTARY
A) beneficial   B) healthy   C) wholesome   D) curative   E) harmful

7. SATIATE
A) satisfy   B) starve   C) sate   D) glut   E) gorge

8. HOT-HEADED
A) angry   B) irritable   C) fiery   D) hot-tempered   E) composed

D. Synonyms – Spelling

Complete the synonym of the word in **bold**.

1. **resentment**   bi__te__ne__s

2. **healthy**   vi__oro__s

3. **prepare**   arr__ng__

4. **elegant**   st__li__h

5. **overflow**   o__ers__ill

6. **means**   __eth__d

7. **concrete**   so__i__

Set 45

A. Synonyms in context: Select the correct answer from the options provided.

1. To <u>present</u> the findings
A) show   B) conceal   C) obscure   D) mask   E) veil

2. To <u>knit</u> a sweater
A) unravel   B) weave   C) undo   D) unweave   E) unknit

3. To have a <u>fervor</u> for justice
A) apathy   B) indifference   C) detachment   D) disinterest   E) passion

4. To have a <u>discourse</u> on politics
A) silence   B) discussion   C) stillness   D) calm   E) peace

5. To be <u>analytical</u> in thinking
A) illogical   B) irrational   C) unreasonable   D) absurd   E) logical

6. To jump in a water <u>puddle</u>
A) dry   B) arid   C) parched   D) pool   E) desiccated

7. To <u>smash</u> a vase
A) break   B) fix   C) repair   D) restore   E) heal

8. To have a <u>basin</u> in the bathroom
A) rise   B) ascend   C) sink   D) soar   E) elevate

B. Sentence Completion – Missing Word

Select the correct answer from the options provided.

1. The museum housed a collection of _____ objects from ancient civilizations.
A) living   B) breathing   C) alive   D) inanimate

2. He spent years _____ his skills, becoming a master craftsman.
A) ignoring   B) dismissing   C) neglecting   D) honing

3. The governor adamantly _____ raising taxes that would burden the public.
A) opposes   B) supports   C) concurs with   D) abets

4. The gift was a mere _____ of appreciation, a small gesture of thanks.
A) burden   B) requirement   C) obligation   D) token

5. The future looked _____, filled with uncertainty and hardship.
A) bright   B) hopeful   C) bleak   D) positive

C. Homonyms

From the list below, fill in the blanks.

none	nun	crewel	cruel	jam	foot

1. Disposed to inflict pain or suffering   _____

2. An informal gathering of musicians playing together   _____

3. By no means, not at all   _____

4. A blockage caused by too many vehicles or people   _____

5. A woman belonging to a religious order   _____

6. Devoid of humane feelings   _____

7. The lower extremity of the leg below the ankle   _____

8. Slackly twisted worsted yarn used for embroidery   _____

9. A unit of linear measure equal to 12 inches   _____

10. A group of syllables constituting a metrical unit of a verse   _____

D. Analogies

Select the correct answer from the options provided.

1   DEFINITE is to INDEFINITE as
A) philanthropic is to admired
B) prolific is to celebrated
C) elite is to envied
D) magnificent is to awed
E) certain is to tentative

2   CRUTCHES are to MOBILITY as
A) imbalance is to fast
B) hearing aid is to audition
C) braille is to comprehension
D) subtitle is to hear
E) communication is to language

3   VEHICLE is to SEDAN as
A) melody is to song
B) alphabet is to language
C) galaxy is to eat
D) building is to skyscraper
E) orchestra is to symphony

4   VENERABLE is to REVERED as
A) despised is to scorned
B) succinct is to rambling
C) exactly is to roughly
D) focused is to random
E) direct is to labyrinthine

Set 46

A. Synonyms

Select the word that most closely matches the meaning of the word provided.

1. EARSPITTING
A) quiet   B) silent   C) soft   D) muted   E) deafening

2. REPLICA
A) original   B) copy   C) genuine   D) unique   E) real

3. SOPHISTICATED
A) common   B) coarse   C) vulgar   D) ordinary   E) classy

4. INUNDATE
A) flood   B) dry   C) dehydrate   D) parch   E) desiccate

5. RISKY
A) safe   B) secure   C) hazardous   D) sure   E) reliable

6. HARDSHIP
A) ease   B) comfort   C) prosperity   D) difficulty   E) happiness

7. DISREGARD
A) heed   B) ignore   C) respect   D) attend   E) value

8. MYRIAD
A) countless   B) limited   C) scarce   D) finite   E) measurable

B. Sentence Completion - Double Blanks

Select the correct answer from the options provided.

1. The court's decision set a dangerous _____ that could have far-reaching _____ for individual rights and freedoms.

A) resolution...conclusion   B) exception...deviation   C) precedent...consequences   D) ambiguity...clarity

2. The water _____ from the mountain spring, crystal clear and _____.

A) polluted...dirty   B) stagnant...still   C) flowed...pure   D) artificial...manmade

3. The teacher _____ the student for his disruptive behavior, demanding an _____ and a promise to improve his conduct.

A) lauded...praised   B) ignored...dismissed   C) encouraged...motivated   D) scolded...apology

4. He was completely _____ by her charm and wit, falling deeply in love with her almost _____.

A) smitten...instantly   B) repelled...dispirited   C) indifferent...uninvolved   D) irritated...annoyed

C. Antonyms

Pick the word that means the opposite or near opposite of the word provided.

1. STUBBORNNESS
   A) obstinacy   B) flexibility   C) persistence   D) rigidity   E) tenacity

2. YEARNING
   A) longing   B) desire   C) craving   D) disinterest   E) aspiration

3. IMPERVIOUS
   A) resistant   B) permeable   C) unaffected   D) impregnable   E) invulnerable

4. OPPRESSIVE
   A) tyrannical   B) liberating   C) cruel   D) unbearable   E) suffocating

5. RECIPROCATE
   A) return   B) exchange   C) repay   D) requite   E) withhold

6. POPULOUS
   A) crowded   B) dense   C) populous   D) teeming   E) deserted

7. PIETY
   A) sinfulness   B) reverence   C) religion   D) faith   E) holiness

8. ELICIT
   A) draw   B) suppress   C) extract   D) provoke   E) induce

D. Synonyms – Spelling

Complete the synonym of the word in **bold**.

1. **propose**   su__ges__

2. **pillage**   pl__nd__r

3. **embed**   __mp__ant

4. **principle**   t__n__t

5. **succession**   s__que__ce

6. **budget**   e__on__mi__al

7. **deceive**   mi__le__d

Set 47

A. Synonyms in context: Select the correct answer from the options provided.

1. To have a <u>deluge</u> of emails
A) drought   B) dryness   C) flood   D) shortage   E) lack

2. To <u>enunciate</u> words clearly
A) mumble   B) pronounce   C) mutter   D) whisper   E) murmur

3. To <u>convoke</u> a meeting
A) dismiss   B) cancel   C) summon   D) postpone   E) defer

4. To <u>clutch</u> the door knob
A) set free   B) slacken   C) decline   D) release   E) grip

5. To <u>yield</u> the right of way
A) take   B) seize   C) give   D) snatch   E) claim

6. To <u>coddle</u> your child
A) neglect   B) ignore   C) disregard   D) overlook   E) pamper

7. To <u>commiserate</u> with a friend
A) sympathize   B) ridicule   C) scorn   D) deride   E) jeer

8. To have a <u>royal</u> legacy
A) modest   B) diffident   C) humble   D) regal   E) unassertive

B. Sentence Completion – Missing Word

Select the correct answer from the options provided.

1. Her fascination with the _____ led her down a path of secret rituals and forbidden knowledge.
A) science   B) occult   C) religion   D) history

2. A strong _____ in literacy and numeracy is essential for success in life.
A) foundation   B) degree   C) diploma   D) certificate

3. He felt a wave of _____ for the suffering child, wishing he could do more to help.
A) sympathy   B) antipathy   C) annoyance   D) indifference

4. The job was _____, both physically and mentally, leaving him drained at the end of each day.
A) rewarding   B) relaxing   C) taxing   D) stimulating

5. He swore to _____ his family from any harm, dedicating his life to their safety.
A) abandon   B) threaten   C) ignore   D) protect

C. Homonyms

From the list below, fill in the blanks.

right	beat	beet	write	fly	seal

1.   To form words by inscribing characters   _____

2.   To express in literary form   _____

3.   To move through the air   _____

4.   To travel in an aircraft or a spacecraft   _____

5.   The opposite of "left"   _____

6.   A semiaquatic mammal that lives in cold climates   _____

7.   A red root vegetable   _____

8.   An embossed emblem used for authentication   _____

9.   To defeat or strike someone   _____

10. Being in accordance with what is just, good, or proper   _____

D. Analogies

Select the correct answer from the options provided.

1   INFLATION is to PRICE INCREASE as
A)   drought is to crop failure
B)   knowledge is to intellectual stagnation
C)   pioneering is to despondency
D)   suppression is to censorship
E)   melancholy is to innovation

2   PROLIFIC is to PRODUCTIVE as
A)   expansive is to abbreviate
B)   passionate is to indifferent
C)   barren is to sterile
D)   exuberant is to restrain
E)   radiant is to obscure

3   SWOLLEN is to SHRUNK as
A)   inarticulate is to alienating
B)   dormant is to obsolete
C)   enlarged is to reduced
D)   stingy is to detrimental
E)   apathetic is to draining

4   CHEETAH is to FAST as
A)   mole is to rustle
B)   whisper is to burrow
C)   eagle is to blaze
D)   star is to soar
E)   turtle is to slow

Set 48

A. Synonyms

Select the word that most closely matches the meaning of the word provided.

1. DEFENSIVE
A) offensive   B) aggressive   C) careless   D) protective   E) vulnerable

2. TICKLE
A) bore   B) amuse   C) irritate   D) vex   E) displease

3. DETECT
A) miss   B) overlook   C) discover   D) conceal   E) hide

4. REAP
A) sow   B) harvest   C) scatter   D) waste   E) squander

5. AWAKE
A) alert   B) drowsy   C) unconscious   D) dormant   E) inactive

6. DIFFER
A) agree   B) match   C) conform   D) coincide   E) vary

7. MORALE
A) depression   B) spirit   C) gloom   D) apathy   E) discouragement

8. TELEPATHIC
A) blind   B) psychic   C) ignorant   D) skeptical   E) doubtful

B. Sentence Completion - Double Blanks
Select the correct answer from the options provided.

1. After years of neglect, the historical building was finally undergoing extensive _____ to restore it to its _____ glory.

A) destruction...ruin   B) repair...former   C) neglect...desolation   D) rebuilding...alteration

2. The young child's mind was still _____ and _____ to new ideas and experiences.

A) rigid...unyielding   B) critical...judgmental   C) developed...mature   D) malleable...open

3. The investigation was _____, leaving no stone unturned and ensuring that all possible leads were _____ .

A) complete...pursued   B) hasty...premature   C) flawed...biased   D) incomplete...inadequate

4. He excelled in sports and other _____ activities, demonstrating a high level of fitness and _____.

A) intellectual...mental   B) emotional...sensitive   C) physical...agility   D) artistic...creative

C. Antonyms

Pick the word that means the opposite or near opposite of the word provided.

1. RECONNAISSANCE
A) exploration   B) ignorance   C) observation   D) inspection   E) investigation

2. CONSISTENT
A) steady   B) constant   C) coherent   D) varying   E) reliable

3. DOCUMENT
A) record   B) report   C) conceal   D) paper   E) evidence

4. PROLIFERATION
A) reduction   B) growth   C) expansion   D) multiplication   E) spread

5. AUTOMATIC
A) mechanical   B) computerized   C) streamlined   D) manual   E) robotized

6. FLOURISH
A) grow   B) expand   C) sprout   D) mushroom   E) decline

7. RELEASE
A) detain   B) liberate   C) discharge   D) emit   E) unleash

8. NOVELTY
A) innovation   B) originality   C) familiarity   D) curiosity   E) uniqueness

D. Synonyms – Spelling

Complete the synonym of the word in **bold**.

1. **lash**   str__k__

2. **parental**   fam__li__l

3. **erratic**   ir__egul__r

4. **humorous**   a__us__ng

5. **muddle**   co__fu__e

6. **outshine**   s__rpa__s

7. **deterrent**   pr__ven__ive

Set 49

A. Synonyms in context: Select the correct answer from the options provided.

1. To <u>exonerate</u> an accused
A) accuse   B) blame   C) clear   D) convict   E) sentence

2. To have <u>renown</u> for a skill
A) obscurity   B) fame   C) insignificance   D) infamy   E) disgrace

3. To be <u>graceful</u> in a dance
A) clumsy   B) awkward   C) ungainly   D) elegant   E) ungraceful

4. To watch a puppy <u>snuggle</u>
A) cuddle   B) shove   C) thrust   D) repel   E) reject

5. To <u>pace</u> the room restlessly
A) sit   B) rest   C) relax   D) recline   E) walk

6. To be <u>insular</u> in views
A) open   B) narrow   C) outgoing   D) friendly   E) cosmopolitan

7. To <u>lure</u> someone with a trap
A) repulse   B) disgust   C) deter   D) dissuade   E) bait

8. To experience the <u>drudgery</u> of a job
A) pleasure   B) enjoyment   C) toil   D) fun   E) recreation

B. Sentence Completion – Missing Word

Select the correct answer from the options provided.

1. The corporation was accused of _____ its workers, paying them low wages and denying them basic rights.
A) appreciating   B) recognizing   C) valuing   D) exploiting

2. He prided himself on his _____, keeping his workspace meticulously organized and tidy.
A) messiness   B) neatness   C) disorganization   D) sloppiness

3. Only citizens who are _____ to vote can cast their ballots in the election.
A) ineligible   B) unqualified   C) disqualified   D) eligible

4. He felt the need to _____ himself of the negative thoughts and emotions that were weighing him down.
A) purge   B) embrace   C) indulge   D) ignore

5. She was meticulous in _____ the furniture, ensuring each piece was perfectly placed.
A) arranging   B) disarranging   C) scattering   D) dismantling

C. Homonyms

From the list below, fill in the blanks.

main	mane	buy	by	Maine	bye

1. Long hair growing about the neck and head of some mammals _____

2. To acquire possession, ownership, or rights _____

3. The most important or central part of something _____

4. To obtain in exchange for something _____

5. A principal pipe or line in a utility system like electricity _____

6. A farewell _____

7. In proximity to something _____

8. The bribe someone _____

9. A state in the northeastern United States _____

10. Advance to the next round without playing an opponent _____

D. Analogies

Select the correct answer from the options provided.

1   FLOWER is to ROSE as
A)   orion is to constellation
B)   summer is to season
C)   desert is to landscape
D)   tree is to oak
E)   jalapeño is to pepper

2   HUNTER is to RIFLE as
A)   keyboard is to pianist
B)   fisherman is to rod
C)   compass is to navigator
D)   screwdriver is to screw
E)   microscope is to biologist

3   EQUIVOCAL is to AMBIGUOUS as
A)   shadowy is to luminous
B)   breakable is to unyielding
C)   clear-cut is to definitive
D)   needy is to self-sufficient
E)   guarded is to open

4   RELUCTANT is to EAGER as
A)   hesitant is to willing
B)   shadowy is to ill-defined
C)   fence-sitting is to neutral
D)   crystalline is to clear
E)   rehearsed is to deliberate

Set 50

A. Synonyms

Select the word that most closely matches the meaning of the word provided.

1. THROWBACK
A) innovation   B) novelty   C) modernity   D) advancement   E) relic

2. IMPLORE
A) command   B) beg   C) demand   D) refuse   E) reject

3. ENDORSE
A) prohibit   B) condemn   C) approve   D) oppose   E) veto

4. PROVENANCE
A) origin   B) end   C) result   D) effect   E) outcome

5. CLERGY
A) laity   B) laymen   C) secular   D) priests   E) profane

6. BRAKE
A) accelerate   B) stop   C) go   D) continue   E) proceed

7. SPURIOUS
A) true   B) genuine   C) authentic   D) false   E) real

8. EASYGOING
A) agitated   B) relaxed   C) restless   D) stormy   E) violent

B. Sentence Completion - Double Blanks

Select the correct answer from the options provided.

1. The _____ of the remote village lived a simple life, _____ by the hustle and bustle of the modern world.

A) visitor...tourist   B) ruler...governor   C) stranger...outsider   D) dwellers...untouched

2. The author's _____ work ignited a heated debate, with _____ arguments on both sides of the issue.

A) factual...objective   B) humorous...amusing   C) controversial...passionate   D) emotional...touching

3. The planets in our solar system _____ the sun in precise elliptical paths, following the _____ of celestial mechanics.

A) orbit...laws   B) occupy...inhabit   C) collide...crash   D) illuminate...brighten

4. The border dispute escalated into a brief _____ between the two countries, raising fears of a wider _____.

A) quarrel...meeting   B) skirmish...conflict   C) diplomacy...discussion   D) decision...resolution

C. Antonyms

Pick the word that means the opposite or near opposite of the word provided.

1. EXPONENTIAL
A) rapid   B) geometric   C) explosive   D) accelerating   E) linear

2. LECTURE
A) sermon   B) discourse   C) speech   D) listen   E) moral

3. OBLIGATORY
A) optional   B) mandatory   C) required   D) necessary   E) essential

4. FEASIBLE
A) conceivable   B) possible   C) workable   D) impracticable   E) achievable

5. STAUNCH
A) wavering   B) faithful   C) steadfast   D) firm   E) reliable

6. UNSOLICITED
A) unwanted   B) uninvited   C) unsought   D) requested   E) voluntary

7. SERENE
A) calm   B) agitated   C) tranquil   D) placid   E) quiet

8. SHREWDNESS
A) reason   B) logic   C) sense   D) naivety   E) intelligence

D. Synonyms – Spelling

Complete the synonym of the word in **bold**.

1. **shard**   fr__gme__t

2. **purpose**   obj__cti__e

3. **heyday**   c__im__x

4. **distinct**   se__ara__e

5. **gather**   con__e__e

6. **license**   a__pro__al

7. **benefactor** p__tr__n

Set 51

A. Synonyms in context: Select the correct answer from the options provided.

1. To have a vibe of <u>melancholy</u>
A) happiness   B) joy   C) cheerfulness   D) sadness   E) bliss

2. To be <u>indecipherable</u> in expressions
A) obvious   B) clear   C) indistinct   D) evident   E) understandable

3. To <u>plod</u> through the snow
A) glide   B) trudge   C) slip   D) skate   E) slither

4. To be <u>sober</u> after the party
A) drunk   B) intoxicated   C) inebriated   D) abstinent   E) wasted

5. To be <u>affirmative</u> in answers
A) positive   B) doubtful   C) uncertain   D) hesitant   E) dubious

6. To <u>reprimand</u> the employees
A) praise   B) compliment   C) commend   D) scold   E) laud

7. To <u>designate</u> a role
A) reject   B) discard   C) abandon   D) forsake   E) assign

8. To be a <u>knave</u> in dealings
A) hero   B) knight   C) villain   D) noble   E) virtuous

B. Sentence Completion – Missing Word

Select the correct answer from the options provided.

1. He had a unique _____, always doing things a little differently from everyone else.
A) quirk   B) flaw   C) blemish   D) defect

2. The story was a mere _____ of his imagination, a fantastical tale with no basis in reality.
A) figment   B) nonfiction   C) reality   D) biography

3. The castle's _____ corridors and hidden passageways were a maze of confusion and danger.
A) straightforward   B) open   C) labyrinthine   D) spacious

4. The music had a/an _____ effect on his soul, calming his anxieties and bringing him peace.
A) upsetting   B) therapeutic   C) frustrating   D) disturbing

5. The machine's primary _____ was to convert raw materials into finished products.
A) purpose   B) invention   C) product   D) outcome

C. Homonyms

From the list below, fill in the blanks.

hair	board	hare	lead	fan	bored

1. A flat, smooth piece of wood   _____

2. The fine strands that grow from the head of humans   _____

3. A device with rotating blades used to move air   _____

4. A small, long-eared mammal   _____

5. To guide or direct someone or something   _____

6. A group of persons having advisory powers   _____

7. A heavy, ductile, soft gray metal   _____

8. To go aboard something, such as a ship, train, or airplane   _____

9. An enthusiastic admirer of something   _____

10. Feeling uninterested or tired   _____

D. Analogies

Select the correct answer from the options provided.

1   DRENCH is to SOAK as
A) blindfold is to sight
B) antidote is to poison
C) soothe is to irritate
D) saturate is to imbue
E) optimize is to clutter

2   INSIPID is to FLAVORFUL as
A) bland is to tasty
B) glance is to skim
C) disentangle is to free
D) sprinkle is to refresh
E) immerse is to engulf

3   DIAMOND is to HARD as
A) pepper is to cool
B) cucumber is to burn
C) cotton is to soft
D) flutter is to butterfly
E) murmur is to whisper

4   SCALE is to WEIGHT as
A) sunlight is to sundial
B) clock is to time
C) level is to gauge
D) measurement is to ruler
E) magnification is to scope

Set 52

A. Synonyms

Select the word that most closely matches the meaning of the word provided.

1. VENUE
A) nowhere   B) location   C) blank   D) emptiness   E) nothingness

2. FACET
A) whole   B) entirety   C) aspect   D) completeness   E) fullness

3. RUDIMENTARY
A) basic   B) complex   C) elaborate   D) sophisticated   E) intricate

4. EMPATHY
A) indifference   B) apathy   C) compassion   D) cruelty   E) hostility

5. MIST
A) clarity   B) fog   C) brightness   D) lucidity   E) visibility

6. CHALLENGE
A) acceptance   B) agreement   C) approval   D) contest   E) compliance

7. VISAGE
A) back   B) face   C) reverse   D) behind   E) tail

8. TEEMING
A) clear   B) empty   C) free   D) crowded   E) spacious

B. Sentence Completion - Double Blanks
Select the correct answer from the options provided.

1. The ship _____ violently in the rough seas, throwing passengers to the floor and causing _____ and fear.

A) lurched...chaos   B) glide...float   C) dock...moor   D) anchor...stabilize

2. He refused to _____ himself by engaging in such petty and _____ activities.

A) elevate...exalt   B) refine...purify   C) debase...immoral   D) justify...excuse

3. The sudden loud noise _____ her from her sleep, leaving her heart pounding and feeling _____.

A) calmed...soothed   B) amused...entertained   C) comforted...assured   D) startled...disoriented

4. The wild horse was _____ and easily spooked, requiring a gentle and patient approach to gain its _____.

A) calm...docile   B) playful...energetic   C) confident...bold   D) skittish...trust

C. Antonyms

Pick the word that means the opposite or near opposite of the word provided.

1. SUBSERVIENCE
A) obedience   B) subordination   C) deference   D) dominance   E) servility

2. INCANDESCENT
A) bright   B) dim   C) radiant   D) brilliant   E) luminous

3. BESTOW
A) deprive   B) grant   C) confer   D) present   E) award

4. INTERN
A) trainee   B) apprentice   C) student   D) novice   E) manager

5. SMUG
A) self-satisfied B) humble   C) arrogant   D) conceited   E) smug

6. CULTIVATE
A) neglect   B) develop   C) improve   D) nurture   E) foster

7. MOTIVATE
A) inspire   B) encourage   C) stimulate   D) discourage   E) influence

8. MALCONTENT
A) unhappy   B) satisfied   C) discontented   D) rebellious   E) disgruntled

D. Synonyms – Spelling

Complete the synonym of the word in **bold**.

1. **distract**   d__ve__t

2. **retaliation**   re__en__e

3. **languid**   sl__g__ish

4. **badger**   h__r__ss

5. **unique**   sin__ula__

6. **bump**   col__id__

7. **basis**   g__ou__d

Set 53

A. Synonyms in context: Select the correct answer from the options provided.

1. To put on a <u>spectacle</u>
A) concealment   B) display   C) secrecy   D) cover   E) veil

2. To have <u>virtuousness</u> in character
A) wickedness   B) evil   C) sin   D) vice   E) goodness

3. To <u>heed</u> the advice
A) ignore   B) listen   C) neglect   D) overlook   E) forget

4. To <u>douse</u> the sponge
A) dry   B) dehydrate   C) parch   D) soak   E) wither

5. To <u>enhance</u> a photo
A) improve   B) degrade   C) deteriorate   D) impair   E) damage

6. To see the <u>emergence</u> of a new technology
A) disappearance   B) vanishing   C) appearance   D) hiding   E) concealment

7. To have <u>zoning</u> for the land
A) unification   B) division   C) combination   D) fusion   E) merger

8. To be <u>servile</u> to a master
A) rebellious   B) defiant   C) resistant   D) disobedient   E) submissive

B. Sentence Completion – Missing Word

Select the correct answer from the options provided.

1. He presented a/an _____ argument, logically and convincingly supporting his position.
A) flawed   B) cogent   C) incoherent   D) unpersuasive

2. She had a strange _____ of impending doom, a feeling that something terrible was about to happen.
A) reverie   B) memory   C) dream   D) premonition

3. The first _____ he made after receiving his inheritance was a new car.
A) peculiar   B) erratic   C) purchase   D) scarce

4. The protesters were _____ from the building for causing a disturbance.
A) invited   B) welcomed   C) expelled   D) admitted

5. The once lively party had become _____ and subdued.
A) riotous   B) exuberant   C) dismal   D) festive

C. Homonyms

From the list below, fill in the blanks.

groan	pen	cell	sell	grown	pool

1. An instrument for writing or drawing with ink _____

2. To give something to someone in exchange for money _____

3. A small room in a prison _____

4. A deep, low sound expressing pain or disappointment _____

5. A small enclosure for animals _____

6. Persuade someone on the merits of something _____

7. Become larger or greater over time _____

8. An artificial or natural body of water _____

9. A group made by combining resources, money, etc. _____

10. A single unit of an organism _____

D. Analogies

Select the correct answer from the options provided.

1   CONIFER is to PINE as
A)   grass is to wheat
B)   carnivore is to kangaroo
C)   reptile is to frog
D)   lichen is to mushroom
E)   marsupial is to rabbit

2   TODDLE is to WALK as
A)   rustle is to crackle
B)   twinkle is to shine
C)   mumble is to speak
D)   fizzle is to explode
E)   nibble is to drink

3   SEEK is to DISCOVER as
A)   mislead is to guide
B)   deceive is to direct
C)   befoul is to purify
D)   search is to find
E)   exploit is to cultivate

4   EMBEZZLE is to DONATE as
A)   sketch is to outline
B)   misappropriate is to contribute
C)   attempt is to try
D)   translate is to interpret
E)   decipher is to understand

Set 54

A. Synonyms

Select the word that most closely matches the meaning of the word provided.

1. EMINENT
A) obscure   B) unknown   C) insignificant   D) distinguished   E) ordinary

2. CRITERIA
A) standards   B) anomalies   C) deviations   D) irregularities   E) variations

3. PROBE
A) ignore   B) investigate   C) neglect   D) disregard   E) dismiss

4. CYNICISM
A) optimism   B) faith   C) trust   D) skepticism   E) confidence

5. DEFT
A) clumsy   B) awkward   C) inept   D) incompetent   E) skillful

6. PANICKY
A) scared   B) courageous   C) bold   D) fearless   E) heroic

7. GUISE
A) reality   B) truth   C) honesty   D) disguise   E) genuineness

8. UNFASTEN
A) tighten   B) loosen   C) fasten   D) bind   E) attach

B. Sentence Completion - Double Blanks

Select the correct answer from the options provided.

1. The reporter _____ the politician's words, _____ their meaning and creating a major public controversy.

A) clarified...explain   B) accurately...reported   C) misquoted...twisting   D) brief...paraphrased

2. The clown's silly _____ delighted the children, filling the room with _____ and joy.

A) solemnity...seriousness   B) antics...laughter   C) anger...frustration   D) sadness...grief

3. She received an _____ performance evaluation, recognized for her exceptional _____, dedication, and contributions to the team.

A) average...mediocre   B) failing...insufficient   C) average...mediocre   D) outstanding...skills

4. The disease had become a _____ on the community, affecting countless lives and causing widespread _____.

A) blight...suffering   B) blessing...benefit   C) remedy...cure   D) miracle...improvement

C. Antonyms

Pick the word that means the opposite or near opposite of the word provided.

1. DEFAULT
A) fail   B) payment   C) forfeit   D) omit   E) evade

2. CLAMOROUS
A) quiet   B) loud   C) vociferous   D) boisterous   E) uproarious

3. ZONE
A) area   B) region   C) section   D) whole   E) territory

4. INCOME
A) earnings   B) revenue   C) salary   D) profit   E) expense

5. ROUND UP
A) enclose   B) gather   C) confine   D) release   E) herd

6. ETCH
A) inscribe   B) speak   C) engrave   D) carve   E) stamp

7. SWIFT
A) quick   B) speedy   C) slow   D) hassled   E) accelerated

8. IRRADIATE
A) illuminate   B) lighten   C) brighten   D) illustrate   E) obscure

D. Synonyms – Spelling

Complete the synonym of the word in **bold**.

1. **moderate**   t__m__er__te

2. **twisting**   wi__di__g

3. **mock**   d__rid__

4. **waive**   ren__un__e

5. **triviality**   i__sig__ific__nce

6. **unconscionable**   u__re__so__able

7. **dappled**   spo__t__d

ANSWERS
and
EXPLANATIONS

Set 1: Answers

A. Synonyms in context
1. pivot	2. imitate	3. equilibrium	4. enliven	5. condense
6. absurd	7. abuse	8. dependent		

B. Sentence Completion – Missing Word
1. flagging	2. despise	3. dreary	4. patronage	5. disruptive

C. Homonyms
1. yard	2. heal	3. yard	4. arm	5. flee
6. arm	7. arm	8. flea	9. yard	10. heel

D. Analogies
1. D- jocund and cheerful both mean happy and lighthearted. Gloomy and sullen both mean sad and dark.

2. B- both pairs of words are antonyms of each other: candor is the opposite of evasion, just as transparent is the opposite of opaque.

3. E- a wheel is a part of a car, just as a sail is a part of a ship. They have a correct part:whole relation.

4. C- an infection can cause fever, just as a trauma can cause shock. They have a correct cause-and-effect relation.

Set 2: Answers

A. Synonyms
1. desert	2. kind	3. brief	4. varied	5. arrogant
6. remedy	7. grammar	8. breeze		

B. Sentence Completion - Double Blanks
1. B	2. A	3. D	4. B

C. Antonyms
1. noncompulsory	2. dump	3. pointless	4. joy	5. smile
6. erase	7. delay	8. darken		

D. Synonyms – Spelling
1. herald	2. expedite	3. appeal	4. disgusting	5. unable
6. tempo	7. sentence			

Set 3: Answers

A. Synonyms in context
1. eccentric	2. aesthetic	3. rage	4. allegory	5. defective
6. activate	7. inheritance	8. responsible		

B. Sentence Completion – Missing Word
1. gibberish	2. conceit	3. hesitant	4. livid	5. scoop

C. Homonyms
1. faun	2. fawn	3. fawn	4. hole	5. whole
6. flu	7. flue	8. hole	9. whole	10. fawn

D. Analogies
1. D- vaccines are used to immunize from disease, just as bandages are used to protect wounds. They have an object-purpose relationship.
2. C- foxes are known to be cunning, just as owls are known to be wise. They have a correct defining characteristic relationship.
3. E- austere and harsh both mean severely strict or stern, just as gentle and tender both mean mildly soft or kind. Both pairs of words are synonyms of each other.
4. A- ascending refers to rising up, while descending refers to falling down. Both pairs of words are antonyms of each other.

Set 4: Answers

A. Synonyms
1. rave	2. tempt	3. vista	4. intuition	5. squelch
6. boring	7. honest	8. miserable		

B. Sentence Completion - Double Blanks
1. A	2. C	3. D	4. C

C. Antonyms
1. charge	2. appreciate	3. increase	4. emptiness	5. harmful
6. weaken	7. consider	8. knowing		

D. Synonyms – Spelling
1. mistrust	2. postpone	3. irritable	4. danger	5. coating
6. itemize	7. difficulty			

Set 5: Answers

A. Synonyms in context
1. disaster	2. immaculate	3. collapse	4. vegetation	5. criticize
6. wrap	7. gun	8. safeguard		

B. Sentence Completion – Missing Word
1. failing	2. sloshed	3. riveted	4. garbled	5. jaunty

C. Homonyms
1. coarse	2. course	3. sail	4. sail	5. peal
6. coarse	7. peel	8. sale	9. sale	10. course

D. Analogies
1. B- affinity is the opposite of aversion, just as attraction is the opposite of repulsion. Both pairs of words are antonyms of each other.
2. E- a touchscreen is a part of a smartphone, just as a monitor is a part of a computer. They have a correct part to whole relationship.
3. C- overwatering can cause rotting in plants, just as underfeeding can cause stunted growth. They both have a correct cause-and-effect relationship.
4. D- a misconception and a fallacy are both false or misleading arguments, just as accuracy and precision both refer to exactness and correctness. Both pairs of words are synonyms of each other.

Set 6: Answers

A. Synonyms
1. lethal	2. cause	3. discord	4. blissful	5. snivel
6. curt	7. truth	8. distort		

B. Sentence Completion - Double Blanks
1. B	2. D	3. B	4. C

C. Antonyms
1. well- accustomed	2. obscure	3. withdraw	4. stupidity	5. narrow
6. rallied	7. jump	8. conformist		

D. Synonyms – Spelling
1. disregard	2. ponder	3. crack	4. conciseness	5. equipment
6. impersonator	7. eliminate			

Set 7: Answers

A. Synonyms in context
1. provoke	2. mesmerize	3. flap	4. spiteful	5. radiant
6. disgrace	7. dormancy	8. suit		

B. Sentence Completion – Missing Word
1. animated	2. regrettable	3. unyielding	4. checkup	5. befell

C. Homonyms
1. one	2. paws	3. well	4. well	5. won
6. one	7. tie	8. pause	9. won	10. tie

D. Analogies
1. C- microscopes are used to closely examine small things, just as telescopes are used to observe distant objects. They have a correct object-purpose relationship.
2. D- a downpour is a heavy precipitation, just as a gale is a strong wind-air movement. They have a correct general-to-specific relationship.
3. A- serene and tranquil mean calm and peaceful, just as chaotic and disorderly mean uncontrolled and disorganized. Both pairs of words are synonyms of each other.
4. C- fickle means frequently changing, steadfast means resolutely constant, while flexible means willing to change, and rigid means not changeable. Both pairs of words are antonyms of each other.

Set 8: Answers

A. Synonyms
1. document	2. shimmering	3. front	4. disprove	5. dash
6. wither	7. fix	8. demand		

B. Sentence Completion - Double Blanks
1. A	2. C	3. D	4. B

C. Antonyms
1. hate	2. mend	3. trivial	4. occupy	5. failure
6. disgrace	7. heal	8. temporary		

D. Synonyms – Spelling
1. period	2. difficult	3. rebuke	4. timely	5. break
6. deplete	7. advantage			

Set 9: Answers

A. Synonyms in context
1. surplus	2. remember	3. stung	4. devote	5. flammable
6. giant	7. range	8. isolate		

B. Sentence Completion – Missing Word
1. overwrought	2. arrival	3. lithe	4. timid	5. linguistics

C. Homonyms
1. strike	2. steal	3. elicit	4. bank	5. bank
6. illicit	7. steel	8. strike	9. bank	10. strike

D. Analogies
1. C- referees use whistles, just as painters use brushes. They both have the user-to-tool relationship, which the other options lack.
2. C- gregarious and sociable mean outgoing and friendly, just as aloof and withdrawn mean reserved and introverted. Both pairs of words are synonyms of each other
3. B- a seedling precedes a sapling in plant growth, just as a caterpillar precedes a chrysalis in butterfly development. They have a correct sequence relationship.
4. A- audacious means daring or adventurous while timid means lacking courage, just as bold means unafraid, while cowardly means fearful. Both pairs of words are antonyms of each other.

Set 10: Answers

A. Synonyms
1. block	2. renewal	3. undead	4. healthy	5. burdensome
6. silly	7. evident	8. grand		

B. Sentence Completion - Double Blanks
1. D	2. D	3. C	4. A

C. Antonyms
1. flexible	2. succumb	3. splice	4. certain	5. rude
6. copy	7. nonmonetary	8. extravagance		

D. Synonyms – Spelling
1. approval	2. dwelling	3. complaint	4. danger	5. capably
6. emulate	7. indifference			

Set 11: Answers

A. Synonyms in context
1. moody	2. abundantly	3. chatter	4. beat	5. curl
6. scanty	7. lazy	8. religious		

B. Sentence Completion – Missing Word
1. ash	2. implementation	3. defaced	4. dank	5. falter

C. Homonyms
1. weather	2. stick	3. idle	4. whether	5. stick
6. idyll	7. stick	8. idol	9. idol	10. stick

D. Analogies
1. E- a wing is part of an airplane, just as a rudder is part of a boat. They have a correct part-to-whole relationship.
2. B- fervent and zealous mean passionate and enthusiastic, just as Indifferent and apathetic mean unconcerned and lacking interest. Both pairs of words are synonyms of each other
3. A- drought causes increased dry aridity, just as floods lead to land erosion. They have a correct cause-and-effect relationship.
4. D- generous means giving freely, while stingy means unwilling to share. Similarly, selfless prioritizes others' needs, while greedy prioritizes one's own. Both pairs of words are antonyms of each other.

Set 12: Answers

A. Synonyms
1. persistent	2. tell	3. stubborn	4. wealthy	5. retreat
6. incapable	7. stain	8. hostile		

B. Sentence Completion - Double Blanks
1. B	2. D	3. A	4. B

C. Antonyms
1. fragile	2. dishonorable	3. whisper	4. secondary	5. unified
6. approve	7. difference	8. refute		

D. Synonyms – Spelling
1. strange	2. beneficial	3. spontaneous	4. disapproval	5. distressed
6. category	7. relief			

Set 13: Answers

A. Synonyms in context
1. spurt	2. boring	3. chaos	4. flawlessness	5. bulge
6. lenient	7. habitual	8. disobey		

B. Sentence Completion – Missing Word
1. commanded	2. stretched	3. mouthpiece	4. squeal	5. lush

C. Homonyms
1. serial	2. tide	3. cereal	4. stamp	5. tied
6. serial	7. serial	8. bat	9. stamp	10. bat

D. Analogies
1. E- flippant treats serious matters lightly, while solemn treats them with seriousness. Similarly, irreverent means irreligious, while pious adheres strictly to religious or moral principles. Both pairs of words are antonyms of each other.
2. C- alpacas produce wool, just as geese produce down feathers. They have a correct functional relationship.
3. E- a peach is a type of drupe fruit, just as a peanut is a type of legume plant. They have a correct general-to-specific relationship.
4. D- persistent and tenacious mean stubborn and persistent in effort, just as fleeting and ephemeral mean short-lived and temporary. Both pairs of words are synonyms of each other.

Set 14: Answers

A. Synonyms
1. list	2. modest	3. strange	4. explain	5. daze
6. anger	7. praise	8. venture		

B. Sentence Completion - Double Blanks
1. A	2. D	3. B	4. B

C. Antonyms
1. trash	2. imprudent	3. cheerful	4. natural	5. optional
6. calm	7. attractive	8. landmark		

D. Synonyms – Spelling
1. submerge	2. reservoir	3. caution	4. emotional	5. profitable
6. earnestly	7. unassuming			

Set 15: Answers

A. Synonyms in context
| 1. allowable | 2. conflict | 3. laugh | 4. grasp | 5. hatch |
| 6. ecstatic | 7. heartfelt | 8. majestic | | |

B. Sentence Completion – Missing Word
| 1. deterrent | 2. daunting | 3. corroborated | 4. solid | 5. dupe |

C. Homonyms
| 1. cede | 2. pact | 3. seed | 4. spring | 5. bear |
| 6. pact | 7. bear | 8. spring | 9. seed | 10. packed |

D. Analogies
1. E- impede and obstruct mean hinder and block progress, just as facilitate and ease mean make something easier to do. Both pairs of words are synonyms of each other.

2. B- chefs use whisks to blend ingredients, just as authors use pens to write. They have a correct user-to-tool relationship.

3. C- candid is open and honest, while dishonest implies wrongdoing. Similarly, truthful avoids deception, while deceitful employs it. Both pairs of words are antonyms of each other.

4. A- a lynx is a specific type of feline, just as a wombat is a specific type of marsupial. They have a correct general-to-specific relationship.

Set 16: Answers

A. Synonyms
| 1. lean | 2. contaminated | 3. rude | 4. loom | 5. gorgeous |
| 6. grumpy | 7. diversion | 8. unfinished | | |

B. Sentence Completion - Double Blanks
| 1. C | 2. C | 3. D | 4. A |

C. Antonyms
| 1. confuse | 2. direct | 3. powerlessness | 4. proven | 5. minor |
| 6. effective | 7. satisfied | 8. impossible | | |

D. Synonyms – Spelling
| 1. sneak | 2. appeal | 3. pinch | 4. require | 5. courage |
| 6. spread | 7. convene | | | |

Set 17: Answers

A. Synonyms in context
1. eternal	2. related	3. inadequate	4. relaxed	5. adviser
6. ponder	7. make up	8. hinder		

B. Sentence Completion – Missing Word
1. furrow	2. teeming	3. punishment	4. ruminating	5. vague

C. Homonyms
1. berth	2. weak	3. birth	4. week	5. birth
6. sound	7. sound	8. bill	9. bill	10. weak

D. Analogies
1. D- impertinent shows a lack of respect, while respectful shows due consideration. Similarly, insolent behaves rudely or arrogantly, while courteous shows politeness and consideration. Both pairs of words are antonyms of each other.

2. A- a pixel is the smallest unit of an image, just as a note is the smallest unit of a melody. They have a correct part-to-whole relationship.

3. B - sunburn is caused by excessive exposure to the sun's ultraviolet rays, just as hypothermia is caused by exposure to cold temperatures. They have a correct cause-and-effect relationship.

4. C- melodious and harmonious mean pleasant and pleasing to the ear. Noisy and discordant mean harsh and unpleasant to the ear. Both pairs of words are synonyms of each other.

Set 18: Answers

A. Synonyms
1. skill	2. summon	3. stubborn	4. review	5. retaliation
6. doubt	7. target	8. noisy		

B. Sentence Completion - Double Blanks
1. B	2. C	3. A	4. B

C. Antonyms
1. urban	2. naive	3. impartial	4. opening	5. build
6. condemn	7. withdraw	8. conclusion		

D. Synonyms – Spelling
1. avoid	2. smoke	3. reduction	4. continue	5. unplanned
6. disappoint	7. sprout			

Set 19: Answers

A. Synonyms in context
1. remove	2. fate	3. transient	4. exaggeration	5. unfriendly
6. wicked	7. error	8. support		

B. Sentence Completion – Missing Word
1. outwit	2. dismount	3. immature	4. endless	5. coexist

C. Homonyms
1. bough	2. pale	3. bow	4. inn	5. bow
6. bow	7. pail	8. bow	9. in	10. inn

D. Analogies
1. A- hammers are used for pounding, just as screwdrivers are used for turning screws. They have a correct object-to-purpose relationship.
2. E- vigilant pays close attention to potential dangers, while complacent is unconcerned. Similarly, alert is quick to notice, while inattentive is lacking in focus. Both pairs of words are antonyms of each other.
3. A- vacant and empty mean devoid of contents or occupants, just as occupied and full mean having contents or occupants. Both pairs of words are synonyms of each other.
4. B- football is a specific type of sport, just as chess is a specific type of a board game. They have a correct general-to-specific relationship.

Set 20: Answers

A. Synonyms
1. urge	2. impression	3. control	4. perfume	5. obscure
6. materialism	7. orderly	8. stick		

B. Sentence Completion - Double Blanks
1. A	2. D	3. C	4. D

C. Antonyms
1. comprehend	2. endanger	3. dystopia	4. careless	5. botanical
6. bore	7. objective	8. full		

D. Synonyms – Spelling
1. sparkle	2. maintain	3. diminish	4. persevere	5. touching
6. inclined	7. dissent			

Set 21: Answers

A. Synonyms in context
1. cause	2. hoarder	3. independent	4. explore	5. dull
6. varied	7. defamatory	8. departure		

B. Sentence Completion – Missing Word
1. strident	2. torpid	3. remnant	4. employ	5. reactivate

C. Homonyms
1. set	2. made	3. yoke	4. maid	5. yolk
6. book	7. set	8. book	9. book	10. set

D. Analogies
1. E- both the key and the switch serve as control mechanisms for their respective objects—the key opens the lock, while the switch turns on the light. They have a correct object-and-function relationship.

2. C- scientists conduct experiments to gather evidence and test hypotheses, just as historians document historical events and people. They have a correct performer-and-action relationship.

3. A- concise expresses ideas clearly, while rambling is long-winded. Similarly, precise is exact and accurate, while vague is unclear or ambiguous. Both pairs of words are antonyms of each other.

4. D- mild and gentile both describe a gentle or calm temperament, while fierce and brutal represent extreme aggression or violence. Both pairs of words are synonyms of each other.

Set 22: Answers

A. Synonyms
1. border	2. cup	3. grunt	4. dictatorship	5. unite
6. cowardly	7. clear	8. restricted		

B. Sentence Completion - Double Blanks
1. C	2. B	3. A	4. D

C. Antonyms
1. detach	2. pacify	3. airtight	4. misleading	5. feebleness
6. fairness	7. cause	8. concealment		

D. Synonyms – Spelling
1. defective	2. assemble	3. procrastinate	4. satisfy	5. glorify
6. repeat	7. dangerous			

Set 23: Answers

A. Synonyms in context
1. intention	2. loyalty	3. clarify	4. giggle	5. detonate
6. tired	7. pure	8. revel		

B. Sentence Completion – Missing Word
1. spasmodic	2. sweeping	3. stolid	4. lively	5. augment

C. Homonyms
1. rapt	2. real	3. case	4. wrapped	5. case
6. case	7. real	8. reel	9. case	10. rap

D. Analogies
1. B- fragile and delicate both indicate vulnerability or susceptibility to damage, while sturdy and robust signify strength and resilience. Both pairs of words are synonyms of each other.
2. C- excessive exercise causes muscle soreness, just as overeating causes a stomachache. They have a correct cause-and-effect relation.
3. E- children are naive and lack experience while adults are experienced and have a good understanding of the world. They have a correct degree of difference relationship.
4. A- mercurial is prone to changes, while steadfast is firm. Similarly, volatile is easily changed, while stable is consistent. Both pairs of words are antonyms of each other.

Set 24: Answers

A. Synonyms
1. impose	2. unmatched	3. stain	4. experiment	5. cellar
6. drive	7. fragrant	8. disparity		

B. Sentence Completion - Double Blanks
1. B	2. D	3. A	4. A

C. Antonyms
1. facilitate	2. submissive	3. ignore	4. brave	5. exit
6. unpleasant	7. achievable	8. conviction		

D. Synonyms – Spelling
1. reliability	2. relevant	3. footnote	4. pause	5. laughable
6. message	7. placate			

Set 25: Answers

A. Synonyms in context
1. slander	2. audacity	3. erase	4. reject	5. stress
6. carve	7. idle	8. sentimental		

B. Sentence Completion – Missing Word
1. fondness	2. edgy	3. improvise	4. surrender	5. equipment

C. Homonyms
1. plain	2. jamb	3. plane	4. scale	5. rose
6. plane	7. plane	8. jam	9. rose	10. scale

D. Analogies
1. A- pollution causes ecological damage just as deforestation causes habitat loss for many species. They have a correct cause-and-effect relationship.

2. B- jovial is full of good humor and enjoyment, while morose is sullen and depressed. Similarly, cheerful is optimistic and upbeat, while downcast is pessimistic and gloomy. Both pairs of words are antonyms of each other.

3. E- lucid and clear both describe clarity and ease of understanding, while murky and obscure represent confusion and difficulty in comprehension. Both pairs of words are synonyms of each other.

4. B- a dictionary helps define words, just as a thesaurus helps find synonyms. They have a correct object-to-purpose relationship.

Set 26: Answers

A. Synonyms
1. separate	2. deter	3. speed	4. slush	5. clearness
6. production	7. ignite	8. pull		

B. Sentence Completion - Double Blanks
1. B	2. C	3. D	4. A

C. Antonyms
1. excitement	2. benefit	3. absence	4. necessity	5. extinguish
6. bold	7. alienate	8. significant		

D. Synonyms – Spelling
1. cluster	2. fugitive	3. bargain	4. provisions	5. cringe
6. inacceptable	7. declaration			

Set 27: Answers

A. Synonyms in context
1. tremor   2. question   3. entirety   4. arrangement   5. ragged
6. exemplify   7. conceal   8. involve

B. Sentence Completion – Missing Word
1. express   2. beside   3. soporific   4. minuscule   5. insufferable

C. Homonyms
1. hall   2. haul   3. scene   4. seen   5. clip
6. clip   7. date   8. haul   9. scene   10. date

D. Analogies
1. C- programmers use code to write computer programs, just as writers use words to write stories, essays, and other texts. They have a correct functional relationship.
2. D- deserts are very dry and receive very little rainfall, just as rainforests are very humid and receive a lot of rainfall. They have a correct defining characteristic relationship.
3. E- ostentatious desires to attract attention, while modest avoids it. Similarly, flashy is showy and attention-seeking, while understated is subtle and unassuming. Both pairs of words are antonyms of each other.
4. A- flimsy and frail both describe a lack of strength or substance, while solid and substantial signify strength and importance. Both pairs of words are synonyms of each other.

Set 28: Answers

A. Synonyms
1. survive   2. heal   3. collect   4. indifferent   5. subtlety
6. submerge   7. vaporize   8. assign

B. Sentence Completion - Double Blanks
1. C   2. A   3. C   4. A

C. Antonyms
1. improvise   2. absence   3. flat   4. silence   5. dissuade
6. sense   7. stride   8. union

D. Synonyms – Spelling
1. endanger   2. amazed   3. discharge   4. preservation   5. decrease
6. nitpick   7. possible

Set 29: Answers

A. Synonyms in context
1. consistency	2. profundity	3. breathe out	4. leave	5. misname
6. fear	7. fight	8. literally		

B. Sentence Completion – Missing Word
1. assumed	2. promontory	3. optional	4. setting	5. callousness

C. Homonyms
1. wait	2. cite	3. deck	4. deck	5. weight
6. site	7. deck	8. sight	9. deck	10. sight

D. Analogies
1. C- dogmatic adheres to a belief, while open-minded considers different viewpoints. Similarly, stubborn resists change, while flexible adapts to new situations. Both pairs of words are antonyms of each other.
2. E- tantalizing and tempting both evoke a strong desire or attraction, while repulsive and revolting cause disgust and aversion. Both pairs of words are synonyms of each other.
3. A- a thermometer is used to measure temperature. a speedometer is used to measure speed. They have a correct object-to-purpose relationship.
4. A- a leaf is part of a plant, just as a petal is part of a flower. They have a correct part-to-whole relationship.

Set 30: Answers

A. Synonyms
1. clothing	2. sign	3. worth	4. implication	5. end
6. copy	7. proverb	8. sharp		

B. Sentence Completion - Double Blanks
1. D	2. B	3. D	4. B

C. Antonyms
1. quiet	2. defender	3. astute	4. healthy	5. praise
6. shrink	7. appreciate	8. fallible		

D. Synonyms – Spelling
1. crude	2. motion	3. improper	4. ballot	5. clutch
6. hobble	7. thrust			

Set 31: Answers

A. Synonyms in context
1. hobby	2. clumsy	3. first	4. eager	5. purify
6. sensible	7. resolve	8. intolerant		

B. Sentence Completion – Missing Word
1. mutiny	2. appointed	3. luxurious	4. regret	5. vegetate

C. Homonyms
1. shear	2. rock	3. roomer	4. sheer	5. rock
6. sheer	7. rumor	8. fall	9. fall	10. sheer

D. Analogies
1. B- smoking is a known risk factor for developing lung cancer, similar to how sugar is a major contributor to diabetes. They have a correct cause-and-effect relationship.
2. A- meticulous and careful both describe attention to detail, while reckless and haphazard represent a lack of attention. Both pairs of words are synonyms of each other.
3. C- impudent shows disrespect, while respectful shows due consideration. Similarly, rude is discourteous, while polite is considerate. Both pairs of words are antonyms of each other.
4. D- the spine provides structure and support to the body, just as the frame provides rigidity and shape to a car. They have a correct part-to-whole relationship.

Set 32: Answers

A. Synonyms
1. reprimand	2. criticism	3. silence	4. castaway	5. stained
6. damage	7. irrational	8. whole		

B. Sentence Completion - Double Blanks
1. C	2. D	3. A	4. B

C. Antonyms
1. frail	2. submissive	3. honesty	4. assemble	5. impassive
6. calm	7. glance	8. peace		

D. Synonyms – Spelling
1. quench	2. difficulty	3. bravery	4. bored	5. instrument
6. slight	7. overpower			

Set 33: Answers

A. Synonyms in context
1. appearance	2. rhythm	3. anxiety	4. forecast	5. healing
6. equal	7. reply	8. enthusiasm		

B. Sentence Completion – Missing Word
1. approving	2. variations	3. site	4. interval	5. bitterness

C. Homonyms
1. genes	2. jeans	3. road	4. rowed	5. rode
6. road	7. ring	8. ring	9. ring	10. ring

D. Analogies
1. B- a hand is part of a clock, just as a needle is part of a syringe. They have a correct part-to-whole relationship.
2. E- verbose and wordy both use excessive words, while concise and succinct convey meaning clearly and with few words. Both pairs of words are synonyms of each other.
3. D- fire leaves ashes behind after it is extinguished, and wound leaves scar behind after it is healed. They have a correct cause-and-effect relationship.
4. A- pragmatic focuses on what is practical, while dreamy focuses on fantasies. Similarly, practical deals with the real world, while idealistic concentrates on unrealized goals. Both pairs of words are antonyms of each other.

Set 34: Answers

A. Synonyms
1. survive	2. lie	3. encourage	4. mournful	5. rage
6. consider	7. weaken	8. agree		

B. Sentence Completion - Double Blanks
1. A	2. B	3. C	4. D

C. Antonyms
1. realistic	2. arrive	3. boss	4. guesswork	5. optional
6. enchant	7. stubborn	8. motivate		

D. Synonyms – Spelling
1. instinct	2. fanatic	3. supervisor	4. release	5. compel
6. authorize	7. javelin			

Set 35: Answers

A. Synonyms in context
1. relentless   2. stamp   3. agreement   4. cheeky   5. invincible
6. diverse   7. rude   8. overenthusiastic

B. Sentence Completion – Missing Word
1. epitome   2. staid   3. outburst   4. rushed   5. insight

C. Homonyms
1. hoard   2. peddle   3. hoard   4. right   5. point
6. pedal   7. pedal   8. right   9. horde   10. point

D. Analogies
1. C- jolly is the opposite of grim, just like bright is the opposite of dim. Both pairs of words are antonyms of each other.
2. A- convivial and friendly both describe a warm and welcoming personality, while impolite and hostile represent unfriendly and aggressive behavior. Both pairs of words are synonyms of each other.
3. B- doctors use stethoscopes as a medical tool, just as carpenters use saws as a woodworking tool. They have a correct user-to-tool relationship.
4. D- Monday comes before Tuesday weekly, just as January comes before February yearly. They have a correct sequence relationship.

Set 36: Answers

A. Synonyms
1. stubborn   2. understand   3. gloomy   4. detailed   5. wink
6. refuge   7. flawless   8. obey

B. Sentence Completion - Double Blanks
1. C   2. B   3. A   4. C

C. Antonyms
1. subtle   2. release   3. virtue   4. approve   5. decisive
6. calmness   7. hide   8. obedience

D. Synonyms – Spelling
1. variation   2. doubtful   3. tiresome   4. supreme   5. scarcity
6. distracted   7. murky

Set 37: Answers

A. Synonyms in context
1. solve	2. pleasure	3. overview	4. monologue	5. abnormal
6. discover	7. charity	8. hint		

B. Sentence Completion – Missing Word
1. dizzy	2. vacillated	3. trembled	4. lackadaisical	5. reptile

C. Homonyms
1. roll	2. bark	3. role	4. note	5. roll
6. fine	7. role	8. barque	9. note	10. fine

D. Analogies
1. D- expressive and articulate both describe fluency, while inarticulate and tongue-tied represent difficulty in communication. Both pairs of words are synonyms of each other.
2. A- abundant is available in large numbers, while scarce is difficult to find. Similarly, plentiful is easily available, while rare is not found often. Both pairs of words are antonyms of each other.
3. E- a verse is part of a poem, just as a scene is part of a play. They have a correct part-to-whole relationship.
4. C- adding heat to water makes it boil just like adding heat to ice makes it melt. They have a correct cause-and-effect relationship.

Set 38: Answers

A. Synonyms
1. uneasy	2. weakness	3. elicit	4. natural	5. trap
6. behaviorism	7. recover	8. request		

B. Sentence Completion - Double Blanks
1. D	2. B	3. C	4. A

C. Antonyms
1. unrepentant	2. ridge	3. enemy	4. ordinary	5. damage
6. pleasant	7. disappear	8. serious		

D. Synonyms – Spelling
1. express	2. position	3. ailment	4. debatable	5. regular
6. prevalent	7. dilemma			

Set 39: Answers

A. Synonyms in context
1. show	2. joyful	3. contempt	4. suppress	5. catch
6. relaxed	7. hungry	8. divide		

B. Sentence Completion – Missing Word
1. belligerent	2. fortitude	3. glib	4. expunge	5. lodged

C. Homonyms
1. horse	2. hoarse	3. mean	4. net	5. plumb
6. mean	7. mean	8. net	9. plum	10. net

D. Analogies
1. E- a spoon is used for eating, just as a knife is used for slicing. They have a correct object-to-purpose relationship.
2. D- honey is characterized by sweetness, just as pepper is characterized by spiciness. They have a correct defining characteristic relationship.
3. C- both pairs of words are antonyms of each other: involuntary is the opposite of voluntary, just as forced is the opposite of chosen.
4. B- both pairs of words are synonyms of each other, and mean to look forward to something that is going to happen.

Set 40: Answers

A. Synonyms
1. casual	2. toxicity	3. haven	4. divert	5. splendor
6. imagine	7. leave	8. hearing		

B. Sentence Completion - Double Blanks
1. B	2. D	3. B	4. C

C. Antonyms
1. last	2. normality	3. friendship	4. conclude	5. confirmation
6. intolerable	7. noncommercial	8. hoard		

D. Synonyms – Spelling
1. thoughtful	2. shoddy	3. bearable	4. theory	5. allude
6. marginal	7. terrified			

Set 41: Answers

A. Synonyms in context
1. distress	2. end	3. hidden	4. tire	5. dispute
6. irregular	7. outline	8. happy		

B. Sentence Completion – Missing Word
1. persistent	2. essential	3. remedy	4. conveyance	5. dungeon

C. Homonyms
1. some	2. stationary	3. match	4. sum	5. light
6. stationery	7. stationary	8. match	9. light	10. sum

D. Analogies
1. E- opalescent and dull are opposite qualities or conditions of appearance, while colorful and drab are opposite qualities or conditions of color. Both pairs of words are antonyms of each other.
2. B- pedantic and nitpicking focus on minute details and rules, while casual and laid-back are relaxed and informal. Both pairs of words are synonyms of each other.
3. C- English is a language, just as guitar is an instrument. They have a correct general-to-specific relationship.
4. A- farmers use plows to till the soil, just as miners use pickaxes to break rocks. They have a correct user-to-tool relationship.

Set 42: Answers

A. Synonyms
1. ancestry	2. life story	3. manipulator	4. wander	5. fold
6. cry	7. follower	8. permanent		

B. Sentence Completion - Double Blanks
1. D	2. A	3. C	4. D

C. Antonyms
1. hurry	2. fresh	3. colorless	4. positive	5. rare
6. honest	7. liable	8. avoid		

D. Synonyms – Spelling
1. appoint	2. exclusion	3. criticize	4. satisfy	5. control
6. element	7. disappear			

Set 43: Answers

A. Synonyms in context
1. sloppy	2. storehouse	3. narcissist	4. aggressive	5. perplex
6. charm	7. scribble	8. discard		

B. Sentence Completion – Missing Word
1. redundant	2. attempt	3. disallowed	4. moribund	5. slick

C. Homonyms
1. naught	2. mousse	3. mousse	4. moose	5. not
6. knot	7. letter	8. letter	9. knot	10. letter

D. Analogies
1. B- exercise is the physical training that strengthens your body, just as reading is the mental activity that stimulates your brain. They have a correct cause-and-effect relationship.
2. D- shush and shout are opposite commands or actions, while silence and noise are opposite states or qualities of being noiseless or noisy. Both pairs of words are antonyms of each other.
3. E- vindicate and clear both defend or exonerate someone from blame, while condemn and censure express strong disapproval. Both pairs of words are synonyms of each other.
4. A- a flashlight reveals hidden details in the dark, just as a translator clarifies the meaning of unfamiliar language. They have a correct object-and-purpose relationship.

Set 44: Answers

A. Synonyms
1. harmony	2. persistent	3. join	4. renew	5. precise
6. carefree	7. caution	8. enhance		

B. Sentence Completion - Double Blanks
1. A	2. D	3. A	4. B

C. Antonyms
1. include	2. birth	3. solo	4. conceal	5. surge
6. harmful	7. starve	8. composed		

D. Synonyms – Spelling
1. bitterness	2. vigorous	3. arrange	4. stylish	5. overspill
6. method	7. solid			

Set 45: Answers

A. Synonyms in context
1. show	2. weave	3. passion	4. discussion	5. logical
6. pool	7. break	8. sink		

B. Sentence Completion – Missing Word
1. inanimate	2. honing	3. opposes	4. token	5. bleak

C. Homonyms
1. cruel	2. jam	3. none	4. jam	5. nun
6. cruel	7. foot	8. crewel	9. foot	10. foot

D. Analogies
1. E- definite and indefinite are opposite conditions of being clear or vague, while certain and tentative are opposite conditions of being sure or unsure. Both pairs of words are antonyms of each other.

2. B- crutches assist with mobility, just as hearing aids assist with hearing (audition). They have a correct object-to-purpose relationship.

3. D- a sedan is a type of vehicle, just as a skyscraper is a type of building. They have a correct general-to-specific relationship.

4. A- venerable and revered are highly respected and admired, while despised and scorned are intensely disliked and looked down upon. Both pairs of words are synonyms of each other.

Set 46: Answers

A. Synonyms
1. deafening	2. copy	3. classy	4. flood	5. hazardous
6. difficulty	7. ignore	8. countless		

B. Sentence Completion - Double Blanks
1. C	2. C	3. D	4. A

C. Antonyms
1. flexibility	2. disinterest	3. permeable	4. liberating	5. withhold
6. deserted	7. sinfulness	8. suppress		

D. Synonyms – Spelling
1. suggest	2. plunder	3. implant	4. tenet	5. sequence
6. economical	7. mislead			

Set 47: Answers

A. Synonyms in context
| 1. flood | 2. pronounce | 3. summon | 4. grip | 5. give |
| 6. pamper | 7. sympathize | 8. regal | | |

B. Sentence Completion – Missing Word
| 1. occult | 2. foundation | 3. sympathy | 4. taxing | 5. protect |

C. Homonyms
| 1. write | 2. write | 3. fly | 4. fly | 5. right |
| 6. seal | 7. beet | 8. seal | 9. beat | 10. right |

D. Analogies
1. A- inflation causes prices to rise, just as drought causes crops to fail. They have a correct cause-and-effect relationship.
2. C- prolific and productive both describe high levels of output or creation, while barren and sterile represent a lack of yield. Both pairs of words are synonyms of each other.
3. C- swollen and shrunk are opposite conditions of being inflated or deflated, while enlarged and reduced are opposite conditions of being increased or decreased. Both pairs of words are antonyms of each other.
4. E- cheetahs are known to be very fast, just as turtles are known to be very slow. They have a correct defining characteristic relationship.

Set 48: Answers

A. Synonyms
| 1. protective | 2. amuse | 3. discover | 4. harvest | 5. alert |
| 6. vary | 7. spirit | 8. psychic | | |

B. Sentence Completion - Double Blanks
| 1. B | 2. D | 3. A | 4. C |

C. Antonyms
| 1. ignorance | 2. varying | 3. conceal | 4. reduction | 5. manual |
| 6. decline | 7. detain | 8. familiarity | | |

D. Synonyms – Spelling
| 1. strike | 2. familial | 3. irregular | 4. amusing | 5. confuse |
| 6. surpass | 7. preventive | | | |

Set 49: Answers

A. Synonyms in context
1. clear	2. fame	3. elegant	4. cuddle	5. walk
6. narrow	7. bait	8. toil		

B. Sentence Completion – Missing Word
1. exploiting	2. neatness	3. eligible	4. purge	5. arranging

C. Homonyms
1. mane	2. buy	3. main	4. buy	5. main
6. bye	7. by	8. buy	9. Maine	10. bye

D. Analogies
1. D- a rose is a type of flower, just as an oak is a type of tree. They have a correct general-to-specific relationship.
2. B- hunters use rifles as a hunting tool, just as fishermen use rods as a fishing tool. They have a correct user-to-tool relationship.
3. C- equivocal and ambiguous are open to multiple interpretations and lacking clarity, while clear-cut and definitive are unambiguous and precise. Both pairs of words are synonyms of each other.
4. A- reluctant and eager are opposite attitudes of being doubtful, while hesitant and willing are opposite attitudes of being resistant. Both pairs of words are antonyms of each other.

Set 50: Answers

A. Synonyms
1. relic	2. beg	3. approve	4. origin	5. priests
6. stop	7. false	8. relaxed		

B. Sentence Completion - Double Blanks
1. D	2. C	3. A	4. B

C. Antonyms
1. linear	2. listen	3. optional	4. impracticable	5. wavering
6. requested	7. agitated	8. naivety		

D. Synonyms – Spelling
1. fragment	2. objective	3. climax	4. separate	5. convene
6. approval	7. patron			

Set 51: Answers

A. Synonyms in context
1. sadness	2. indistinct	3. trudge	4. abstinent	5. positive
6. scold	7. assign	8. villain		

B. Sentence Completion – Missing Word
1. quirk	2. figment	3. labyrinthine	4. therapeutic	5. purpose

C. Homonyms
1. board	2. hair	3. fan	4. hare	5. lead
6. board	7. lead	8. board	9. fan	10. bored

D. Analogies
1. D- drench and soak both mean to wet something thoroughly, just as saturate and imbue both mean to fill something completely. Both pairs of words are synonyms of each other.
2. A- insipid and flavorful are opposite qualities of being tasteless or delicious, while bland and tasty are opposite qualities of being uninteresting or appealing. Both pairs of words are antonyms of each other.
3. C- diamond is a hard material, just as cotton is a soft material. They have a correct defining characteristic relationship.
4. B- a scale allows us to measure and monitor weight, just as a clock enables us to track and tell the time. They have a correct object-to-purpose relationship.

Set 52: Answers

A. Synonyms
1. location	2. aspect	3. basic	4. compassion	5. fog
6. contest	7. face	8. crowded		

B. Sentence Completion - Double Blanks
1. A	2. C	3. D	4. D

C. Antonyms
1. dominance	2. dim	3. deprive	4. manager	5. humble
6. neglect	7. discourage	8. satisfied		

D. Synonyms – Spelling
1. divert	2. revenge	3. sluggish	4. harass	5. singular
6. collide	7. ground			

Set 53: Answers

A. Synonyms in context
1. display	2. goodness	3. listen	4. soak	5. improve
6. appearance	7. division	8. submissive		

B. Sentence Completion – Missing Word
1. cogent	2. premonition	3. purchase	4. expelled	5. dismal

C. Homonyms
1. pen	2. sell	3. cell	4. groan	5. pen
6. sell	7. grown	8. pool	9. pool	10. cell

D. Analogies
1. A- a pine tree is a type of conifer plant, just as wheat belongs to the grass family. They have a correct general-to-specific relationship.
2. C- toddling comes before walking in mobility development, just as mumbling comes before clear speaking in language development. They have a correct sequence relationship.
3. D- seek and search are both actions of looking for something, just as discover and find are both actions of learning or locating something. Both pairs of words are synonyms of each other.
4. B- embezzling and donating are opposite actions of taking or giving money or property, while misappropriating and contributing are opposite actions or activities of using or providing money or property. Both pairs of words are antonyms of each other.

Set 54: Answers

A. Synonyms
1. distinguished	2. standards	3. investigate	4. skepticism	5. skillful
6. scared	7. disguise	8. loosen		

B. Sentence Completion - Double Blanks
1. C	2. B	3. D	4. A

C. Antonyms
1. payment	2. quiet	3. whole	4. expense	5. release
6. speak	7. slow	8. obscure		

D. Synonyms – Spelling
1. temperate	2. winding	3. deride	4. renounce	5. insignificance
6. unreasonable	7. spotted			

Made in the USA
Las Vegas, NV
02 December 2024

13207858R00079